Preface

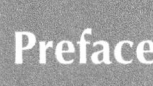

During the initial start-up period of what was then called the Northern Forest Fire Laboratory (or "Fire Lab") in Missoula, Montana, scientists and engineers approached everything from staffing to calibrating new instrumentation to solving fundamental questions about fire behavior as engineering problems—that is to say, they had a beginning, a middle, and a solution at the end. I approached this history of the Fire Lab in a similar fashion, understanding that while research of the Fire Lab's history could continue indefinitely, a "solution" was needed in time for the 50th anniversary celebration on September 18, 2010.

Believing that the Fire Lab's research should be seen in its historical context, I first reviewed existing histories of American forestry research in general and fire research in particular. C.E. (Mike) Hardy's study of Harry Gisborne and early fire research was particularly helpful in this regard, but secondary sources could take me only so far in understanding the Fire Lab's history and its context. So next I turned to primary documents: Forest Service annual reports, correspondence, technical papers, and even photographs. I also had the good fortune of being able to interview many of the Fire Lab's earliest researchers who, with their stellar memories, provided insights and details to help me fill in many of the gaps.

I then integrated all of these components and asked several Fire Lab reviewers to test my results. Their comments, noting my omissions, misinterpretations, and outright mistakes, have been extremely valuable. Indeed, I could not have completed this history without their assistance.

The research conducted at the Fire Lab over the past 50 years has been diverse, complex, and multi-dimensional, involving hundreds of scientists, engineers, skilled technicians, and support personnel. Researchers have focused on everything from fundamental physics to the effects of fire on ecosystems over time, and have examined questions at a variety of scales from the microscopic to satellite images of the earth. Some researchers have looked to the past to understand the history of fire, while others have investigated the effects of fire on global climate change and, thus, on the long-term future of the planet.

With such a diverse body of research, this report can only briefly summarize the achievements of the past 50 years. That said, I hope this history suggests the scope of the ground-breaking research conducted at the Missoula Fire Sciences Laboratory and introduces some of the men and women who have dedicated their professional lives to public service with the goal of better understanding fire and its relationship to our nation's wildlands.

Diane M. Smith, Independent Historian of Science
September 18, 2010
Missoula, Montana

Contents

The Missoula Fire Sciences Laboratory:

A 50-Year Dedication to Understanding Wildlands and Fire

Diane M. Smith

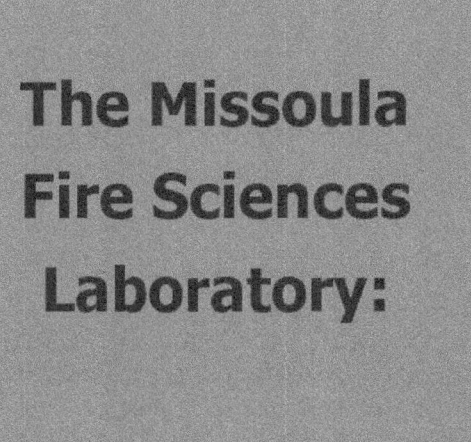

United States Department of Agriculture / Forest Service

Rocky Mountain Research Station
General Technical Report RMRS-GTR-270

March 2012

Abstract

In 1960, the USDA Forest Service established the Northern Forest Fire Laboratory (now the Missoula Fire Sciences Laboratory) to find scientific solutions for better managing the nation's wildland resources and to research ways to improve forest fire prevention and suppression. This new state-of-the-art research facility did not emerge from a vacuum, however. This report explores the tradition of research within the Forest Service and how these early research programs, including fire-related research at the Priest River Experimental Forest, contributed to the establishment of the Fire Lab. This history also explores the role played by key events in shaping fire-related research.

Keywords: wildland fire research, Missoula Fire Sciences Laboratory, Northern Rocky Mountain Research Station, Forest Service history, forest fire prevention and suppression history

INTRODUCTION

The Northern Forest Fire Laboratory is indeed a unique structure. There is probably not another structure like it in the world. The 35,000 square feet of floor space contain scientific research facilities designed specifically to investigate a wide variety of fire problems. When the laboratory is fully equipped, we believe that this will be one of the finest research institutions of its kind. This whole complex of combustion chambers, wind tunnels, radar scopes, and laboratories for physics, chemistry, meteorology, and fuels research will constitute a powerful means for making progress in the big job of forest protection and management (McArdle 1960).

When Forest Service Chief Richard McArdle dedicated the new Northern Forest Fire Laboratory ("Fire Lab") in Missoula, Montana, on September 12, 1960, the Fire Lab became an official part of an agency dedicated to finding scientific solutions for better managing the nation's wildland resources. With its two wind tunnels and state-of-the-art controlled-environment combustion chamber, the Northern Forest Fire Laboratory offered an "economical way to bring about more effective forest fire prevention and suppression" through scientific research (USDA Forest Service 1957).

This new research facility did not emerge from a vacuum, however. Rather, the building and its research programs grew naturally from programs that began with the establishment of the Forest Service in 1905 and the long-standing commitment of Gifford Pinchot, the agency's first Chief Forester, to provide the information needed to make informed decisions about how to protect and manage the nation's forests and other wildlands. Pinchot and his successor, Henry Graves, set the stage for a long tradition of fulltime fire researchers: Harry Gisborne, Jack Barrows, C.E. (Mike) Hardy, Richard Rothermel, Frank Albini, Jim Brown, Patricia Andrews; Stephen Arno, Robert Mutch, and Robert Burgan. A newer generation of researchers followed, including Mark Finney, Emily Heyerdahl, Bob Keane, and Wei Min Hao, along with many others who have advanced the fundamental understanding of fire science. While over the years the problems associated with managing the nation's forests have grown more complex, one question has stayed with the Forest Service since Gifford Pinchot first assumed a leadership role: How can the nation's forests and wildlands best be managed in relationship to fire?

Physical Science Technician, Robert (Bob) Schuette, watches over a test fire in the combustion chamber of the Northern Forest Fire Laboratory in 1967 (*photo: USDA Forest Service*).

Fire effects publications.

An Agency Dedicated to Research

Not long after Gifford Pinchot was hired in 1888 to head what was then known as the Division of Forestry, he initiated a series of research projects. These included studies of North American forests, in cooperation with the U.S. Geological Survey; a survey of the history of forestry in the United States and the "practical application of conservation forest treatment … which is much more frequent than is usually supposed"; a study of reforestation after a fire in Colorado; a "photographic forest description of the United States"; field work on forest fires in several states; and a historical study of forest fires "with the purpose of ascertaining the amount of damage and the true place of fires in the economy of the forest." For this study, researchers reviewed thousands of newspapers and records going back to 1754, and transferred data to a classified card index (USDA 1899).

Under Pinchot, the Forest Service also created a series of forest experiment stations, opening the first in 1908. Within 5 years, six forest research stations were in operation in Arizona, Colorado, New Mexico, Utah, and Idaho, where some of the earliest research into forest fires was conducted. In 1922, Harry Gisborne transferred to Priest River Experiment Station in northern Idaho as the first full-time fire scientist. His research included investigating the relationship between lightning and fires and how to measure and predict weather conditions and other factors that affect fire behavior. After World War II, former military personnel also worked at the Priest River Station, adapting and testing military techniques and technologies to fight fires.

Regardless of the approaches developed and technologies tested, the goal was to put the best minds to work researching solutions in the same spirit in which the agency had worked under Pinchot. And, like Pinchot, these researchers looked at all potential problems facing the nation's forests and natural resources—even the weather—as something that might be understood and managed through scientific methods.

This report documents the history of the Northern Forest Fire Laboratory, later called the Intermountain Fire Sciences Lab, and now known as the Missoula Fire Sciences Laboratory, in Missoula, Montana. The first half of the report places the Fire Lab within the history of the Forest Service, describes the rise of forest research generally, and illustrates the importance of fire research within the Forest Service. The second half focuses on the history of the Fire Lab itself, from its original mission and initial research challenges to current projects and educational efforts.

Several themes emerged researching the history of the Fire Lab and are threaded throughout the report: (1) a commitment to both basic and applied research, (2) a dedication to providing management with the information needed to make decisions based on sound science, and (3) a recognition of the interaction of historical events, public policy, and public opinion that have influenced, and continue to influence, fire research.

1. A commitment to both basic and applied research.

Starting in 1908, the Forest Service established a series of research programs to study timber management, silviculture, stream flow and erosion. In 1911, the Forest Service established the Priest River Experimental Forest in Idaho's northern panhandle. Initially focused on developing better methods for harvesting, thinning, planting, and regenerating trees, Priest River researchers soon turned their attention to better understanding the causes and effects of fire. When Henry (Harry) Gisborne transferred to Priest River in 1922, he initiated the Forest Service's first full-time fire research program. When the need for more fundamental, controlled research became clear, the agency constructed three regional fire research laboratories in the 1960s, including the Fire Lab in Missoula.

2. A dedication to providing management with the information needed to make decisions based on sound science.

From the first review of U.S. forest fire history ordered by Gifford Pinchot in 1899, to Jack Barrows' review in the late 1950s of 36,000 forest fires and their effects, the Forest Service has demonstrated a consistent commitment to understanding the challenges facing fire managers. This commitment continued with the early educational efforts of Richard Rothermel, Frank Albini, Robert Burgan, and Patricia Andrews, and the synthesis of literature (known as the Fire Effects Information System or FEIS) conducted by the FEIS team today. Throughout the last hundred years, Forest Service researchers have worked consistently to develop a better understanding of fire and fire behavior, and have provided the best available knowledge to managers so they could make informed decisions.

3. A recognition of the interaction of historical events, public policy, and public opinion that has influenced, and continue to influence, fire research.

National events and certain large fires, particularly in the Rocky Mountain West, have played a formative role in shaping the public's reaction to forest fires, agency responses, and fire research. From the "Big Blowup" in 1910 to the Russian launch of Sputnik in 1957 and the 1988 fires in Yellowstone National Park, external events have often driven investments in research, helped define and prioritize research, and accelerated public debate about the role of fires in national wildlands.

The Missoula Fire Sciences Laboratory was built on these foundations. This is the story of the Fire Lab's 50-year contributions to the on-going search for understanding of fire behavior and its impacts, especially on wildland ecosystems.

Section I: Brief History of the Forest Service and Fire Research

All photos USDA Forest Service

A Planet Shaped By Fire

Because of their close relationships with fires, western forest ecosystems are considered fire dependent. If we hope to sustain the communities of trees, plants, and animals that characterize these wildland forests, we need to understand the natural role of fire, changes brought about by suppressing fire, and alternatives for restoring some reasonable semblance of the natural fire process (Arno 2002).

Humans have a long history with fire. Native Americans, for example, routinely shaped their environment using fire to clear undergrowth, enhance habitat for food crops and wildlife, and flush animals from densely forested areas. Early European settlers also used fire to clear land and open areas for planting, while sheep and cattle ranchers used fire to improve grazing.

Fire does not require human intervention to impact a landscape. Lightning-caused fire, particularly in the Rocky Mountain West, can sweep across a hillside and transform it over night, leaving what appears to be barren ground, devoid of life. And yet, as Natives and early Anglo settlers understood, the burned-over landscape generates new growth that flourishes from the remains of the fire, growing new grasses, flowers, shrubs, and trees, and creating new habitat for wildlife. According to one writer, removing fire from fire-dependent ecosystems can result in "continents ... covered by climax-stage vegetation: a world of great trees, dark and silent" (Mann 2005).

The positive environmental role of fire has been understood for centuries, but fire also has the potential to destroy property and cultural landmarks and to put lives at risk. As historians Stephen J. Pyne and Samuel P. Hays and ecologist Stephen Arno have all pointed out, early foresters understood the benefits of fire, and yet most political leaders in the early twentieth century believed that the risks to life and property were too high to allow any fires to burn. Thus, national wildlands were to be protected from all threats, including fire. When Theodore Roosevelt signed the legislation creating the Forest Service in 1905, one of the agency's primary goals was to provide complete fire protection to the nation's forests and other wildlands. Looking back with what scientists now know about fire and forest ecology, it is clear this policy risked the health of some of the very ecosystems the agency sought to protect.

Because fire can be both beneficial and fiercely destructive, wildfires have presented a constant challenge to those who manage the nation's wildlands. Knowledge developed through Fire Lab research has contributed to the evolution of fire management policy, and the Fire Lab has responded to the ever-evolving policy by developing new knowledge and tools to help managers meet the challenge.

Fireweed thrives in a stand of lodgepole pine burned one year earlier. This perennial regenerates from underground stems after being top-killed by fire (*photo: Jim Peaco, National Park Service*).

New stands of lodgepole pine flourish 10 years after the 1988 fires in Yellowstone (*photo: Jim Peaco, National Park Service*).

The Greatest Good, for the Greatest Number, in the Long Run

They trusted trained professionals, guided by science, to make the best decisions. Progressives viewed the unregulated destruction of the nation's forests and waterways as an enormous waste and they believed that converting the nation's wealth into vast personal fortunes was undemocratic and immoral. Scientific management was the answer. Government would apply a business-like efficiency to the development of resources and guarantee fair and wise use (Lewis 2006).

In 1890, the American Association for the Advancement of Science lobbied the administration of President Benjamin Harrison to protect the watersheds in the American West by ensuring "the perpetuity of the forest cover on the western mountain ranges…." (Lewis 2006). In 1891, legislators attached a rider to the General Land Law Revision Act giving the President the power to set aside additional public lands "wholly or in part covered with timber or undergrowth, whether of commercial value or not, as public reservations…." (Brinkley 2009).

With this legislation in hand, Harrison created the Yellowstone Park Timberland Reserve to protect land around the southern edge of Yellowstone National Park. Before leaving office in 1893, Harrison created 15 forest reserves of more than 13 million acres to protect western watersheds. His successor, Grover Cleveland, added 5 million more acres but then stopped, seeing "no reason to continue [creating reserves] if the government did not also provide the means for protecting the forest reserves from unlawful entry" (Lewis 2006).

In 1898, the Department of Agriculture appointed Gifford Pinchot to head the Division of Forestry, replacing the German-born and educated forester, Bernhard Fernow. Germany had initiated much of the earliest research in the science of forestry, and Fernow benefited from that training. However, as historian Samuel P. Hays noted, Fernow believed that the Division of Forestry should dispense information and technical advice based on European principles. Fernow had little interest in developing new knowledge through forestry research, according to Hays (Hays 1959, 1975).

Pinchot had been educated at Yale but, because the college did not yet offer training in forestry, he traveled to Europe to further his education. When Pinchot succeeded Fernow as Chief of the USDA Division of Forestry in 1898, Pinchot took a different approach to managing the agency. Indeed, to emphasize his scientific training, one of Pinchot's first acts was to assume the new title of "Chief Forester" to set himself apart from the other division chiefs, whom he viewed as mere administrators (Lewis 2006).

Believing that national forests should be managed for "the greatest good of the greatest number in the long run," the new Chief Forester promoted a scientific approach to managing forests. During his first year, he established a "Section of Special Investigations, a research arm." By 1902, this new section under Pinchot's leadership achieved division status and had 55 employees (Steen 1976, 2004). Early in his tenure as Chief Forester, Pinchot also established experiment stations so that researchers could live and work in the forests they studied, test new management strategies on the ground, and share results with managers working in similar ecosystems. In his history of the Forest Service's Intermountain Research Station, Richard Klade estimates that "as much as 25 percent of Pinchot's early budget [even before the official establishment of the Forest Service] was related to research" (Klade 2006).

While the early investigations under Pinchot's leadership may not qualify as fundamental research by today's definitions, they nonetheless laid the foundation for the programs that followed and, in Klade's assessment, "reflected Pinchot's realization that programs of practical forestry could only succeed if supported by sound information obtained through research efforts." Under Pinchot's leadership, for example, the Santa Rita Range Reserve opened near Tucson, Arizona, in 1903, and the first forest experiment station opened in 1908 at Fort Valley, Arizona. By 1913, the Forest Service operated six experiment stations in five States to conduct research in various ecosystems and areas of interest, from silviculture to erosion control (Klade 2006).

Establishing the Forest Service

Pinchot both created and inspired the modern Forest Service. He established a model of efficient agency management…. An independent study of the Forest Service administration in 1908 paid high tribute to Pinchot's administrative ability. 'Rarely, if ever,' have we 'met a body of men where the average intelligence was so high, or the loyalty to organization and the work so great' (Robbins 1984).

When Pinchot was first hired as Chief Forester in 1898, he worked for the Department of Agriculture, and yet the Department of the Interior technically managed the national forest reserves. Pinchot, therefore, had to coordinate his agency's activities with those of Interior. While he managed to work within this administrative framework, Pinchot believed he would be more effective if responsibility for the nation's forests were not split between two different agencies. When Pinchot's personal friend, Theodore Roosevelt, ascended to the presidency in 1901 after William McKinley's assassination, Pinchot began to advocate for an administrative transfer of the national reserves from Interior to Agriculture, a move Roosevelt supported. In his first annual address (now known as the "State of the Union") in 1901, for example, President Roosevelt put the argument this way:

At present the protection of the forest reserves rests with the General Land Office, the mapping and description of their timber with the United States Geological Survey, and the preparation of plans for their conservative use with the Bureau of Forestry, which is also charged with the general advancement of practical forestry in the United States. These various functions should be united in the Bureau of Forestry, to which they properly belong. The present diffusion of responsibility is bad from every standpoint. It prevents that effective co-operation between the Government and the men who utilize the resources of the reserves, without which the interests of both must suffer. The scientific bureaus generally should be put under the Department of Agriculture (Roosevelt 1901).

Theodore Roosevelt signed this consolidation into law on February 1, 1905 and the Transfer Act, as it became known, paved the way for the official establishment of the Forest Service within the U.S. Department of Agriculture. As historian Stephen J. Pyne has written, "[w]ith control over the national forests, forestry now had a political base; with Gifford Pinchot, its charismatic chief, it had a leader of national stature; and with the invigorated Forest Service, the conservation movement had a Progressive Era exemplar of a technocratic bureau serving the public interest" (Pyne 1997).

But Pinchot's commitment to scientific forestry and Roosevelt's willingness to help him achieve his goals did not end with the 1905 Transfer Act. Roosevelt's predecessors had created 41 forest reserves totaling close to 50 million acres. In his first year as president, Roosevelt added 13 new reserves totaling 15,500,000 acres (Hays 1959, 1975). When Congress tried to stop Roosevelt from creating more reserves in six Western States, Roosevelt set aside an additional 75,000,000 acres, known as the "midnight reserves," before the legislation took effect. As noted by Timothy Egan in his history of the 1910 fires, Pinchot ended up overseeing close to 180 million forested acres and, in the process, "introduced a new term to the public debate—conservation—and it was here to stay. They had shifted oversight of public land from patronage bureaucrats to professional foresters." As Pinchot would note in his diary right after Roosevelt created the midnight reserves: "'I am very happy tonight'" (Egan 2009).

Remembering the Progressive Era

[I]n many ways, the Forest Service was the ultimate Progressive government bureaucracy. It was idealistic young people, trained as scientists, bringing their scientific knowledge to the forest, to the public lands and trying to bring the benefits of those lands to the greatest good of the greatest number for the longest time—that classic Gifford Pinchot utilitarian principle (Cronan 2005).

Historians refer to the period of 1890-1920 as the Progressive Era, during which men like Gifford Pinchot and Theodore Roosevelt believed that social, economic, and environmental problems could and should be solved "by experts who would undertake scientific investigations and devise workable solutions." Thus, when Pinchot assumed leadership of the fledgling Forest Service, he "infused it with a new spirit of public responsibility," and transformed what had been "a coterie of law clerks into a well-trained force fighting for forest protection and more scientific forest management" (Hays 1959, 1975).

Like the founders of the National Park Service, Pinchot believed in managing the nation's forests for both current needs and future generations. While Pinchot and his successors would struggle with finding the balance between the greatest good for the greatest number, Pinchot set a mandate from the beginning that the Forest Service's primary mission was the conservation of the national forests. For his purposes, that meant protecting the forests from fire.

In one of his first publications for the nascent Forest Service, the new Chief Forester described the important role played by public wildlands under the new agency's protection. First and foremost, Pinchot wrote, forests protected the nation's watersheds and needed to be safeguarded to ensure the continuation of this critical function. Next, forest and other wildlands supplied grass for grazing animals and wood for economic development and growth. While Pinchot considered wood production the "least important" of these primary functions, he also understood that the production of timber would grow in importance as the country itself grew. With these contributions in mind, he wrote that the "best way for the Government to promote each of these three great uses is to protect the forest reserves from fire." Without this protection, he argued, even the "most skillful management is of little effect" (Pinchot 1909).

Pinchot clearly understood the beneficial role fire played in preserving forest health. For example, in 1909, he published his *Primer of Forestry, Part II Practical Forestry*, in which he wrote:

When a tract of woodland is destroyed by fire in one of the Rocky Mountain States, it often happens that the seeds of the lodgepole pine are scattered over it by the wind in prodigious numbers. The seeds germinate abundantly, seedlings spring up, and in a very few years a young even-aged forest of lodgepole pine covers the ground. As it grows older fires destroy patches of it here and there, and in time every patch is covered again with a younger generation of even age. After many years the forest which sprang up after the first fire has become broken into a number of even-aged patches without uniformity in size or regular gradations in age (Pinchot 1909).

Even though Pinchot understood the role fire plays in forest ecology, he still needed to convince skeptical lumbermen that a federal agency dedicated to the nation's forests was in their best interest. To this end, Pinchot conducted detailed inquiries into the impacts of forest fires and researched the history of major fires (Hays 1959, 1975). He established fire protection as one of the agency's overarching management goals and primary duties, as indicated in the first *Use of the National Forest Reserves, Regulations and Instructions*:

Officers of the Forest Service, especially forest rangers, have no duty more important than protecting the reserves from forest fires. During dry and dangerous periods all other work should be subordinate. Most careful attention should be given to the prevention of fires. Methods and equipment for fighting them should be brought to the highest efficiency. No opportunity should be lost to impress the fact that care with small fires is the best way to prevent large ones (Pinchot 1905).

The Forest Service's first "Use Book," as it became known, all foresters were required all foresters to "go to and fight every fire he sees or hears of at once, unless he clearly can not reach it, or is already fighting another fire…. The fact that it may not be on his district has no bearing unless he is certain another ranger is there already." Once at the scene of a fire, rangers were required to stay until they extinguished the fire or they were forced to leave to protect their own life. As Pinchot explained no doubt for the benefit of his critics, "[t]he burden of adequate protection cannot well be borne by the State or by its citizens, much as they have to gain, for it requires great outlay of money to support a trained and equipped force, as well as to provide a fund to meet emergencies. Only the Government can do it, and, since the law does not provide effective protection for the public domain only in forest reserves can the Government give the help so urgently needed" (Pinchot 1905).

Conditions on the ground, however, would soon change the way the Forest Service viewed its ability to protect the nation's wildlands. While Henry Graves, who succeeded Pinchot in 1910, continued to be committed to early detection, fire fighting, and fire prevention, it became clear to him that the Forest Service must also focus on research to better understand the causes, effects, and behavior of fire.

Conserving the Nation's Resources

The central thing for which Conservation stands is to make this country the best possible place to live in, both for us and our descendants. It stands against the waste of the natural resources which cannot be renewed, such as coal and iron; it stands for the perpetuation of the resources which can be renewed, such as the food-producing soils and the forests; and most of all it stands for an equal opportunity for every American citizen to get his fair share of benefit from these resources, both now and hereafter (Gifford Pinchot, First Chief Forester, 1910).

Pinchot championed forest conservation and sound science until 1910, when he was forced out of office for opposing the return of public lands "to the very people Roosevelt and Pinchot had battled [against] for the past decade" (Egan 2009).

Theodore Roosevelt and Gifford Pinchot (left to right) (*photo: USDA Forest Service*).

Henry S. Graves, c. 1890 (*photo: USDA Forest Service*).

Changing How the Nation Viewed Wildfires

No single event changes history. No fire, however awesome, can imprint itself on a continent for decades. But a fire can catalyze change that becomes encoded into public sentiment and political bureaucracies, and that is what the Great Fires [of 1910] did. They prompted reforms that affected how fire would come and go on tens of millions of acres.

They brought the Forest Service to a fork in the road and forced it to choose one path over another (Pyne 2001).

The fire season of 1910 forced the relatively new Forest Service to reevaluate all that it thought it knew about managing forests and fires. While the actual numbers vary depending on the source, the fires that swept through Idaho and Montana burned over 3 million acres, killed more than 80 people—most of them firefighters—and cost the Forest Service approximately 1 million dollars to combat. And no one saw it coming.

In spite of dry weather, the fire season in 1910 started out routinely, with some fires sparked by lightning, others started by abandoned campfires and settlers, and still others started by trains. Unlike in other summers, the small fires of 1910 smoldered but did not go out. "As the weeks wore on, the fires crept and swept," historian Stephen J. Pyne has written, merging with one another, while the Forest Service "rounded up whatever men it could beg, borrow, or buy and shipped them into the backcountry. The crews established camps, cut firelines along ridgetops, and backfired. Over and again, one refrain after another, the saga continued of fires contained, of fires escaping, of new trenches laid down" (Pyne 2001). Then came the winds of August 20 and 21, and the fires seemed to explode. Elers Koch, then Supervisor of the Lolo National Forest, vividly recalled the fires:

For two days the wind blew a gale from the southwest. All along the line, from north of the Canadian boundary south to the Salmon, the gale blew. Little fires picked up into big ones. Fire lines which had been held for days melted away under the fierce blast. The sky turned a ghastly yellow, and at four o'clock it was black dark ahead of the advancing flames. One observer said the air felt electric, as though the whole world was ready to go up in spontaneous combustion. The heat of the fire and the great masses of flaming gas created great whirlwinds which mowed down swaths of trees in advance of the flames. In those two terrible days many fires swept thirty to fifty miles across mountain ranges and rivers (Koch n.d.).

Burning millions of acres throughout the region, the fires of 1910 shook the Forest Service's confidence in its ability to respond to fire. When pressed by the *New York Times* about whether or not "human ingenuity, caution, and wealth [could] devise some means of making such horrors impossible," both former Chief Forester Gifford Pinchot and his successor, Chief Forester Henry Graves who was in charge by the time of the 1910 fires, returned the same answer: "No!"

Wallace, Idaho after the fires of 1910 (*photo: USDA Forest Service*).

"This fire," as reported in the *Times*, "resulted from an unusual combination of circumstances. The main causes were the exceptional drought and the high, steady winds that prevailed for a long period preceding the outbreak of fire." But, the paper added, thousands of forest fires can be prevented if caught early, and if they are promptly suppressed. Unfortunately, even though the Forest Service had pressed for more forest rangers and forest guards, the *Times* article continued, "it has usually found Congress stone deaf" (New York Times 1910).

In this case, however, Congress heard the message loud and clear and responded quickly. They appropriated funds for permanent improvements such as roads to increase forest access, support for protective work and fire fighting and, "in case of extraordinary emergency," an appropriation for an additional $1,000,000. The Forest Service set out to prioritize how to make the most of this increased funding to ensure that "the highest possible state of preparedness might be reached and the most effective use made both of the old appropriation and of the increased appropriation available when the new year should begin" (Graves 1912).

As noted by Forest Service historian Terry West, the 1910 fires posed a significant challenge to Graves's leadership, but he saw the public outcry as a positive force (West 1992). These fires, Graves wrote, exerted "an influence which it would be hard to overestimate." Not only did they catalyze the Congressional response, but they also contributed to public awareness of fire safety. Graves hoped that this new awareness would result in less "carelessness, better laws, and more general efforts to combat fires everywhere. The

Forest Service can well afford to have the community critical of its work," he continued, "for the sake of the support to the general cause of fire protection which this state of the public mind gives" (Graves 1912).

Graves's response to the 1910 fires included initiation of a program of scientific research on fire since, if nothing else, the expense of firefighting made research important (West 1992). Taking a systematic, scientific approach, the Forest Service also created what it referred to as "fire protection plans" for a number of national forests, with the goal of eventually creating plans for all forests. As part of the plans, foresters identified those areas most at risk of fire and in the greatest need of protection (that is to say, with highest timber value), and then planned how to locate fire detection and reporting systems, such as lookout points and communications protocols, to ensure an efficient response. They also considered how to get help to a fire quickly and how to keep firefighters supplied wherever they were located (Graves 1912).

The Gisborne Era of Forest Fire Research

The field is so new that we have nothing to help us except our own imagination and what little ingenuity we possess. I've been at this fire research for five years now and, while I'm becoming more and more convinced that there is nothing revolutionary in it, I am also becoming more certain that by better knowledge of details we can tighten up in both pre-vention and suppression very appreciably (Gisborne 1927).

In 1911, the year after the "Big Burn," a new Forest Service experiment station was established at Priest River in the Idaho Panhandle. Four years later, Chief Henry Graves consolidated all the agency's research-related projects into the Forest Service Branch of Research to enable scientists to focus specifically on research. Then, in 1916, Graves issued a directive to all of the experiment stations to add fire research to their work. According to forester C.E. (Mike) Hardy, Graves' "appeal suggested a general program to divide the forest areas into climatic units, [to] study meteorological and climatic conditions, fire rate of spread under various conditions of weather, fuels (duff moisture was mentioned), topography, and cover, and [to] endeavor to predict dangerous conditions." The following year, the Forest Service decided to initiate a project on "the rate of spread of fire and its relation to different weather conditions, site conditions, and variations in cover" (Hardy 1977). The agency no longer wanted to rely solely on anecdotal and historical understanding of wildland fire. Rather, Graves wanted foresters to begin proactively investigating the causes and effects of fire under different conditions.

Following Chief Graves' general instructions, the new Priest River director, Julius Larsen, initiated a program in 1917 to document the moisture in the "duff" (twigs, wood debris, etc.) and surface soil at three locations where weather conditions were measured. Larsen continued this research in 1918 and added a study of the relationship of fires to weather conditions, gathering data from several new weather stations. As promising as this field research appeared, in 1918 Larsen already anticipated the need for a research laboratory where more rigorous experiments could be initiated. According to Hardy, he "realized that some data must come from the laboratory, but was not successful in locating adequate facilities"

(Hardy 1977). In the meantime, though, Larsen joined with another Priest River researcher, W.C. Lowdermilk, in 1920 to investigate fire hazard in relation to logging slash disposal.

These early research programs helped establish the Priest River Experiment Station as one of the nation's leaders in fire-related research (Wellner 1976). As the program grew, the scientists argued for increased support for research on the causes and behavior of fire, analysis of fire data, and even aerial fire control (Hardy 1977). Their calls were answered in the form of a young forester working for the Forest Service in Oregon. In the spring of 1922, Harry T. Gisborne transferred from the Whitman National Forest in Oregon to Missoula, Montana, which served as the Priest River headquarters and winter operations office. As the first professional forester assigned to fire research fulltime, Gisborne established the station's new research priorities: (1) determining and predicting fire danger, and (2) understanding the relation of forest fires to lightning (Wellner 1976). In particular, Gisborne hoped to use fuel and weather conditions to predict fires a few days in advance in order to give managers on the ground time to prepare.

Gisborne also began to investigate how to measure the moisture of fuels, believing that this was another key to predicting fire danger. As his research demonstrated, the higher the moisture content in surface fuels (e.g., needles, twigs, wood debris, etc.), the less likely a fire will burn (Hardy 1977). While he expressed frustration at the number of measurements required to correlate fire danger with fire behavior, his work began to produce results as well as innovative technologies. One example was the duff hygrometer used to measure fuel moisture. This device used "a strand of rattan [fiber] enclosed in a perforated metal tube with the tip laced just under the top of the duff. The rattan stretched or shrunk according the amount of moisture...." The duff hygrometer was eventually abandoned because it was difficult to calibrate and use (Hardy 1977), but it initiated a series of innovative and relatively inexpensive technologies for estimating the moisture in fuels, an issue that continues to be addressed in the Fire Lab today.

Harry T. Gisborne operating a double tripod heliograph, Tip Top Lookout, Wenatchee National Forest, Washington, 1915 (*photo: courtesy of the Forest History Society, Durham, NC*).

Understanding Relationships Between Weather and Fire

The 1910 fire, which consumed over three million acres and killed seventy-eight firefighters, was an event that raised national awareness. Several more moderate fire years during the period of 1910–1920, culminating in the extreme year of 1919, caused the agency to realize that a deliberate, science-based strategy would be needed to both explain and predict fire activity in the western USA, hopefully leading to options by which the number and size(s) could be reduced (Hardy and Hardy 2007).

In the winter of 1923 and into 1924, Gisborne initiated a new area of research: predict the approach of lightning storms and investigate means to control them. In his own words, Gisborne was already on his way to developing "the best system yet devised for predicting the weather." Expressing his frustration with the enormity of the task, however, he wrote: "Wanted: better weather forecasts" (Hardy 1977).

While Gisborne pursued these research interests, in 1926 he also argued that yet more fire research was needed "to discover the fundamental causes and effects [of fire] which vary in such a way as to cause variable demands on the forest protective organization." If researchers could determine the multiple causes and effects of forest fires, then the Forest Service could better assess risk and make more informed decisions about how to allocate resources during both severe and normal fire years, while still providing "adequate protection during the fire seasons that are less dangerous than the average" (Hardy 1977).

In 1929, Gisborne initiated a review of more than 14,000 storm observations. According to C.E. (Mike) Hardy, Gisborne intended to use the results to improve protection from lightning fire by "increased surveillance, knowledge of the difference between the fire-starting storm and the safe storm, and more accurate 36-hour forecasts of storm occurrence" (Hardy 1977). In 1930, Gisborne added yet another research activity: a statistical analysis of fire records to determine the speed and strength of attack needed to successfully control a fire in the region (Wellner 1976).

In spite of all this activity—or because of it—Harry Gisborne still felt constrained by the lack of adequate research facilities. As early as the 1930s, he began to repeat Julius Larsen's 1918 argument for a research laboratory—a facility with an environmentally controlled wind tunnel/forest fuel combustion chamber. "In a problem rendered complex by so many natural variables it is often the least costly and quickest way to take the problem into the laboratory where each factor can be controlled and the results checked by repeated trials with several factors held constant," Gisborne wrote. In particular, Gisborne recommended the following:

This laboratory should consist of a wind tunnel at least 10 or 12 feet in diameter to accommodate fuels of definite moisture content, at any desired slope, wind velocity as desired, and the air held at any selected temperature and humidity. The effect of ridges and canyons on local winds could be determined so that forecasts can be made more accurately. This need should be given high priority.... (Hardy 1977).

Thus, as Hardy clearly demonstrates in his history of the Gisborne Era (1977), the dedication of the Northern Rockies Fire Sciences Lab in 1960 completed a dream that had started with Julius Larsen and the hiring of Harry Gisborne in the early 1920s. And when the Fire Lab wind tunnels were first tested by researchers, they "almost exactly fulfilled the requirements Gisborne described in 1931" (Hardy 1977; Klade 2006).

Applying Fire Danger Rating in the Field

Gisborne systematically, and often singlehandedly, collected information about fire and its endlessly varied environment: fuels, winds, slopes, moisture, climate, weather. His 27-year effort produced quantities of basic data on fire that proved a gold mine for later researchers (Wells 2008).

Harry Gisborne never appeared to be all that interested in abstract knowledge. Rather, he saw his research as a direct result of having lived "in the field in daily contact with field conditions," producing results and putting tools into the hands of those who had to make decisions in the field (Hardy 1977). As colleague Chuck Wellner recalled, Gisborne "focused his research on critical problems of fire control. He expected involvement and help from forest [managers] and they, in turn, expected research results, and they got them" (Wellner 1976).

To achieve usable results, predicting fire spread and improving control strategies, Gisborne needed reliable weather data, so he turned his attention to establishing a number of field measuring stations. According to Jack Barrows, who joined the Priest River research team after WWII, Gisborne felt that fire danger rating is never going to work unless you can have weather stations properly operated and maintained and he held to that concept throughout his career. And he was right. And he was probably one of the best spokesmen for that concept (Barrows 1976).

Harry Gisborne uses an early fire danger meter to predict forest fire activity in the Kaniksu National Forest in 1937 (*photo: courtesy of the Forest History Society, Durham, NC*).

of occurrence and amount of precipitation, wind velocity and direction, temperature, relative humidity, and the frequency and character of lightning storms are all important factors influencing the ignition and subsequent rate of spread of fires (Barrows 1951).

A constant challenge facing early fire researchers was the lack of affordable technologies capable of measuring weather and fuel moisture characteristics needed to accurately predict fire danger in the field. Harry Gisborne, Chuck Wellner, and C.E. (Mike) Hardy all worked on developing relatively inexpensive technologies and methods that would result in accurate readings. One of Gisborne's particularly innovative solutions was the use of an old Pennzoil advertising rotating sign as an anemometer. George Jemison, a fire researcher at Priest River, and his wife calibrated the rotating sign by driving down a road at a given speed and counting the revolutions per minute. Other technologies developed include portable weather instrument shelters and even a weather measurement kit that could be carried on a firefighter's belt.

The 1934 fire season tested Gisborne's ideas. Readings from the Pete King Ranger Station in Idaho indicated extreme fire weather conditions and the potential for a big fire. But when both Gisborne and C.S. Crocker, the acting supervisor of the Selway National Forest, raised the alarm and asked for extra firefighters, no additional funds or personnel were forthcoming. Gisborne's system had yet to prove itself, and "agency administrators were not persuaded by what they felt was, perhaps, either an error in the local fire-danger estimate or an anomaly at a scale too small to warrant additional resources." But the fire danger was indeed high that year, and without additional firefighters standing by or the resources needed to hire them, the Pete King-McLendon Butte fire burned through a quarter of a million acres before winter snows suppressed it (Hardy 2007).

In this case, the weather stations and fire danger rating system Gisborne and his colleagues had developed were literally tested by fire and proved reliable. And like the 1910 fire before it, the Pete King-McLendon Butte fire motivated the Forest Service to reconsider the way it responded to fire danger. As C.E. (Mike) Hardy noted, the reliability of Gisborne's predictions proved to Forest Service managers that the need for "pre-suppression" (standby) crews could also be anticipated. And it demonstrated the importance of better weather data and further research to help predict fire danger and behavior nationwide.

Measuring the Potential Danger for Fire

Weather conditions are of major importance in determining the probable behavior of fires. The time

Portable scales, developed by Harry Gisborne and his colleagues, were used for weighing ponderosa pine moisture indicator sticks in the field (*photo: USDA Forest Service*).

C.E. (Mike) Hardy and "knock-down" weather instrumentation shelter, 1958 (*photo: USDA Forest Service*).

The first Belt Weather Kit was developed by C.E. (Mike) Hardy (*photo: USDA Forest Service*).

Rating Fire Danger

[I]f sufficient data were at hand and properly compiled, some one factor or some convenient combination of factors might be found that would furnish a warning to increase manpower prior to or during fire emergencies. This became a major goal of Gisborne's which finally bore fruit with the use of the first fire danger rating system on the Pete King-McLendon Butte fires of 1934 (Hardy 1977).

Inspired by an early Kodak light meter that adjusted for light, exposure time, and lens opening, Gisborne "began playing around with various devices to put these factors [fuel, wind, and humidity] together and express them into a single numerical rating scheme...." He created a device similar to a slide rule with "fuel moisture percent categories, wind, accumulated days since 0.2 of an inch of rain, visibility in about three categories." He also added a lightning variable. Leaving all the columns and rows blank, he asked field managers and other researchers to fill in the blanks on a scale from one to six based on their experiences. Once Gisborne received all of their estimates, he smoothed out the differences, creating what became the first fire danger meter, a tool to help foresters better prepare for fire management. As A.A. Brown and Wilfred S. Davis wrote, "If fire danger can be measured correctly, much of the effort in fire preparedness can be allocated to the right time and place, the fire organization can be more effectively built up, and surprises can be reduced to a minimum" (Brown and Davis 1939).

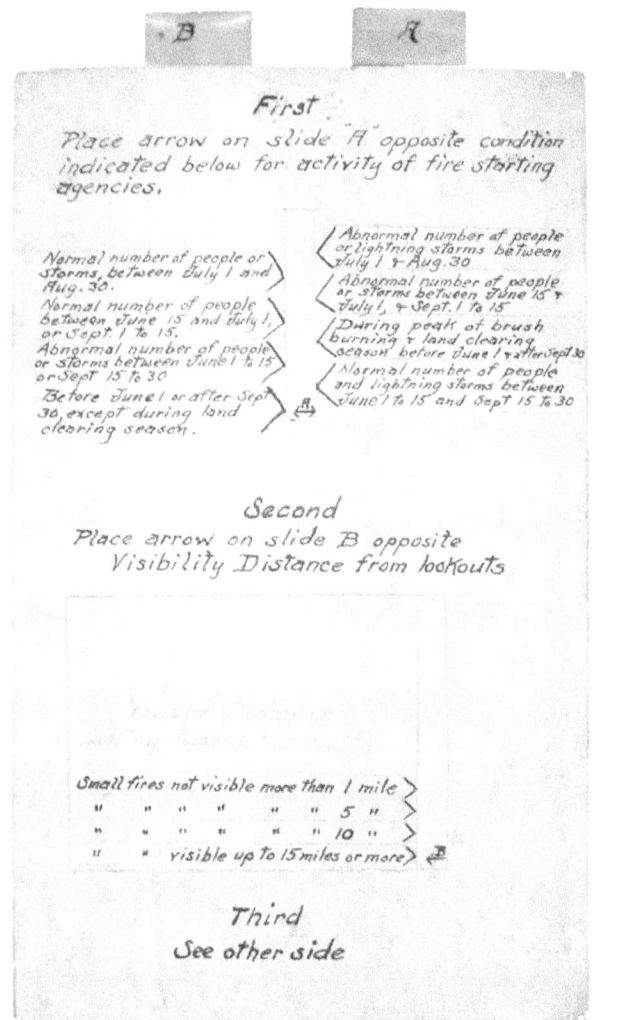
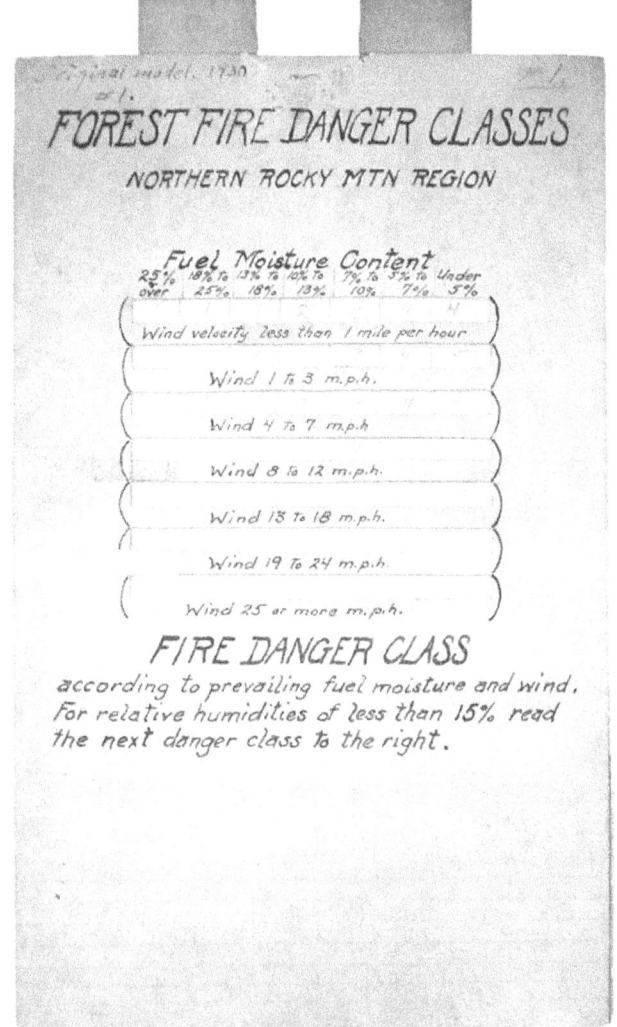

Front (left) and back (right) of Gisborne's original Model One fire danger meter, 1932 (*photo: USDA Forest Service*).

USDA Forest Service RMRS-GTR-270. 2012.

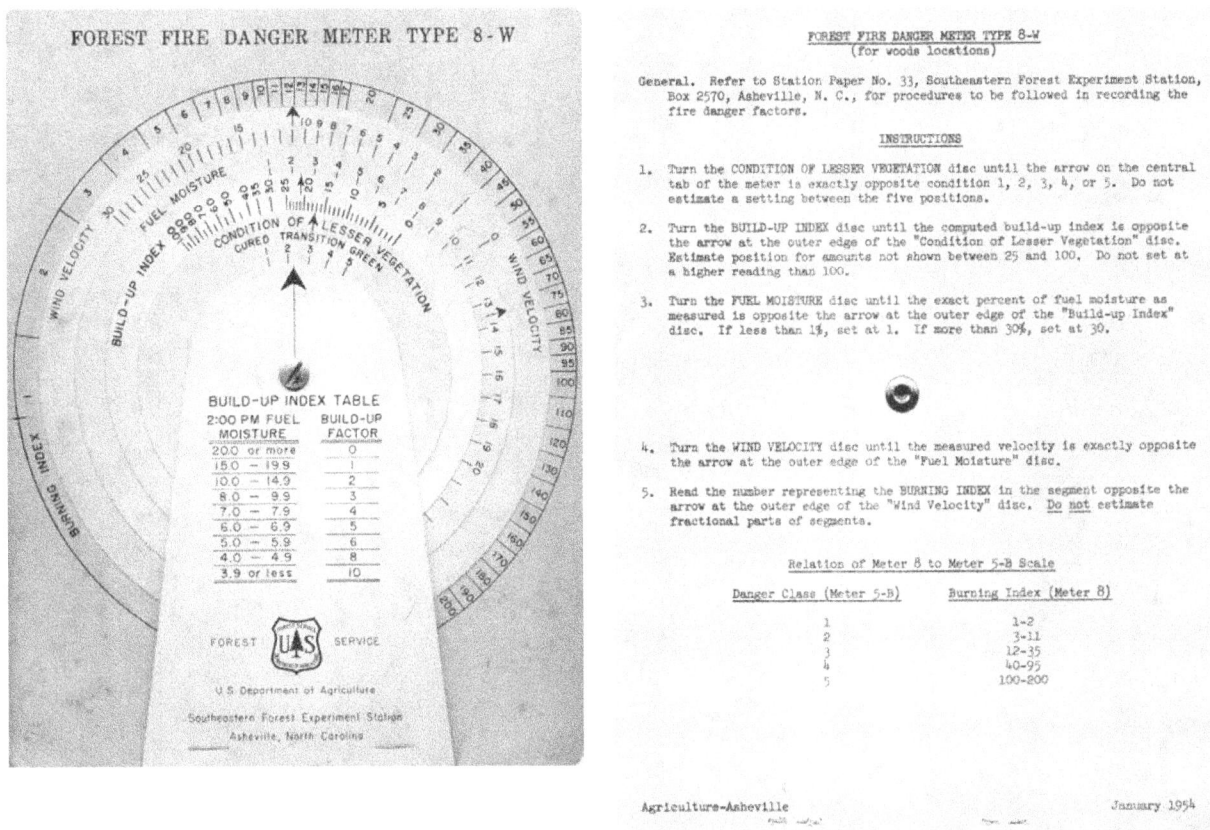

Forest Fire Danger Meter type 8-W, 1954: (a) meter, (b) instructions for use (*photo: courtesy of the Forest History Society, Durham, NC*).

Suppress All Fires by 10 A.M.

The means of fighting forest fires are not everywhere the same, for they burn in many different ways; but in every case the best time to fight a fire is at the beginning, before it has had time to spread. A delay of even a very few minutes may permit a fire that at first could easily have been extinguished to gather headway and get altogether beyond control (Pinchot 1905).

The easiest way to manage fire, particularly those in the "'back-country' of the northern Rockies," was to locate it early and put it out quickly. In 1935 the Forest Service instituted what was then referred to as "the quick-action strategy" to suppress fires (now known as the 10 a m. rule or policy) (Silcox 1935). While on paper this appears a logical solution to suppressing fires, the ruling presented many logistical hurdles, one of which was getting firefighters to the scene of a backcountry fire on time. One innovative response to this problem came in 1940 after successful experiments during the preceding summer in Washington and Montana: the Forest Service began to employ smokejumpers to respond to fires in remote areas. Not having to wait for on-the-ground access, smokejumpers parachuted into the area near a fire and

were often able to contain it quickly. The first 10 years of this program—1940 to 1949—demonstrated the success of this approach to fighting fires in remote areas, with smokejumpers parachuting into 1,424 fires over the 10-year period (Watts 1951). But the 1949 fire season was deadly and provided even more incentive for the Forest Service to learn more about fire behavior to protect the smokejumpers they sent into the line of fire.

On August 5, 1949, a wildfire in the Mann Gulch area of the Helena National Forest, Montana, overran a smokejumper crew that had parachuted into a small valley near the fire. Thirteen men lost their lives, as the fire "blew up" and swept over them (Rothermel 1993). That fall, Harry Gisborne reviewed all available reports on the fire and tried to develop a theory of how the blow-up occurred. Wanting to see the site first hand before winter and determined to learn what lessons could be learned to predict fire behavior and save firefighter lives in the future, he set out to explore the Mann Gulch burn. On November 9, 1949, while hiking through the burned area as part of his investigation, Gisborne had a heart attack and died at the site, in essence the 14th casualty of the fire (Hardy 1977). Gisborne's death could be viewed as the end of an era in fire research but in many ways, it also signaled the beginning of a new one.

Removing bodies from Mann Gulch, August 6, 1949 (*photo: USDA Forest Service*).

Bodies were removed from the site by helicopter and then taken by hearse to Helena (*photo: USDA Forest Service*).

Honoring the Fire Fighters at Mann Gulch

In 1949 the Smokejumpers were still so young that they referred affectionately to all fires they jumped on as 'ten o'clock fires,' as if they already had them under control before they jumped. They were still so young they hadn't learned to count the odds and to sense they might owe the universe a tragedy (Maclean 1992).

The Mann Gulch fire in Montana's Helena National Forest took the lives of 13 men. Their deaths became national news and, according to Richard Rothermel, the Forest Service suffered a severe blow, since it "had not experienced a fatality during a decade of smokejumping and was extremely proud of its elite firefighters" (Rothermel 1993). It also gave fire research proponents additional justification for supporting more rigorous, laboratory-based research.

In 1979, author Norman Maclean contacted Richard Rothermel and Frank Albini at the Fire Lab to help him better understand the fire's behavior for a book he was writing about the Mann Gulch tragedy. As someone who had fought fires himself as a young man, Maclean wanted to know how such a thing could happen. While the Mann Gulch fire left several fire behavior-related questions unanswered, it also left emotional wounds, according to Rothermel. In spite of the event's emotional dimensions—still raw in 1979—Rothermel felt obligated to use his research "to help explain the complicated interactions of fuels, weather, and topography" and to help Maclean better understand what might have happened that day.

Maclean's resulting book, *Young Men and Fire*, published in 1992 after his death, became a popular success, but questions still lingered about what had happened to the young men trapped by the Mann Gulch fire. Using his fire-spread model and other insights into fire behavior, Rothermel addressed some of those questions in his

Mike Hardy (left) and Art Brackebusch at the Wildland Firefighters Memorial, placed on Looking Glass Mountain in Idaho (now Gisborne Mountain) in 1951 (*photo: USDA Forest Service*).

Richard C. Rothermel's publication, *Mann Gulch Fire: A Race That Couldn't Be Won*.

own publication *Mann Gulch Fire: A Race That Couldn't be Won* (1993). He also described how the fire might have spread and why so many young men could not have escaped it.

The Mann Gulch fire led to national support for the kind of research later conducted at the Fire Lab in Missoula. It is also the only known fire event that resulted in both a technical publication and a popular book being published around the same time. Both publications relied, at least in part, on research conducted at the Fire Lab.

Norman Maclean's book, *Young Men and Fire*.

1944 poster featuring Smokey Bear.

Forest Fire Research: A New Generation

The phenomenal growth of fire research during this period from a one-man division (Gisborne) in 1945 to a major forest fire laboratory in 1960 was largely the doing of one man, Jack S. Barrows (Wellner 1976).

As new technologies became available, researchers and fire fighters asked new questions about how to suppress or prevent wildland fires. For example, after World War II, when the Forest Service had greater access to aircraft and surplus military equipment, researchers investigated whether or not techniques developed during the war might be put to use for fighting fires. Characterizing fire as an old enemy and "hostile force" to be battled, they tested the use of aircraft to deliver water and fire retardants. They sought to identify the patterns and concentrations that could be delivered when flying at various speeds and altitudes, the best design characteristics for aerial delivery systems, and the role airplanes and helicopters could and should play in delivery (Pyne 1997). They also worked to identify the best retardant for different fuel types and conditions, to determine how much retardant is needed according to variations in fuels and fire danger, and to predict how long the retardant would be effective (Barrows 1976).

In 1946, after being discharged from the Air Force, forester Jack Barrows joined Harry Gisborne at Priest River. Prior to WWII, Barrows had worked for the National Park Service conducting fire-control training schools throughout the United States. Harry Gisborne often taught at the same training schools, showing students how to use his fire danger rating system. Thus, the two men had a history of working together (Barrows 1976).

As the second fulltime fire researcher at Priest River, Barrows was soon appointed to an experimental research program based in Missoula, Montana, to test the use of World War II bombing techniques to deliver water and retardants to forest fires (Barrows 1976). The partnership between the Forest Service and the U.S. Air Force resulted in a fire-fighting research program that converted aluminum wing tanks into bombs loaded with fire retardants that either exploded mid-air or on impact.

The tests ran from the summer of 1946 through 1947 and confirmed that "fire retardants could be delivered rather precisely to fire targets by aerial bombing techniques." However, the tests also demonstrated that the bombs failed to adequately disperse the retardants. More important for practical application, however, was the conclusion that "aluminum-cased retardant bombs were extremely dangerous to personnel on the ground." Thus, researchers were urged to "explore other types of containers and cascade delivery systems" (Barrows 1971).

Jack Barrows officially initiating the B-29 Superfortress program, which tested the use of water bombs for fighting forest fires (*photo: USDA Forest Service*).

With tests of the aerial bombing of fires concluded, Barrows' next assignment picked up the tradition from Pinchot's time, assessing what could be learned from past experiences with fires. Barrows analyzed data describing 36,000 reported forest fires in the northern Rocky Mountains. As Barrows recalled, Harry Gisborne helped shape the study plan but once they agreed upon a course of action, Gisborne left Barrows to pursue the assigned research according to his own instincts (Barrows 1976).

Like many fire researchers before and after him, Barrows adapted and applied new technology to pursue his research. Using relatively new computer technology, Barrows punched computer cards to describe each fire. His "ability to quickly search for common denominators among the reports allowed him to gain insights that were hidden from earlier researchers...." (Bunton 2000). Barrows's resulting report, "Fire Behavior in Northern Rocky Mountain Forests," published in 1951, made a significant contribution to the analysis of weather and fire behavior over long periods of time. Barrows worked independently on this and other research projects but adopted and followed through on Gisborne's commitment to conducting research that was "application oriented." As

Barrows recalled, they weren't "doing research just for the love of doing research." Rather, Barrows and his colleagues were "working for the field men" who needed access to research results to do their job (Barrows 1976).

Establishing a Division of Fire Research

The Fire Research Program being carried on by the Forest Service is yielding results far beyond expectations from the modest sums invested.... [T]his program] ... is providing knowledge, techniques and equipment for development of more adequate protection of American forests. In addition, the program contributes to the general advancement of basic scientific knowledge.... Fire research needs laboratories equipped with the facilities required in investigation of the difficult technical problems involved in this vital work (Mansfield 1958).

In fiscal year 1949, the Forest Service established a new Division of Fire Research. Its overarching goal was to strengthen the fire-control effort by studying:

The "Forest Service Wing" of the Federal building in Missoula, Montana, corner of Pattee and Pine Streets, 1938. Still headquarters for the Forest Service Northern Region, a limited fire research program started by Harry Gisborne was conducted in the building's basement until 1960 (*photo: USDA Forest Service*).

1. Ways and means of preventing fires;

2. Development of improved fire-fighting equipment, methods, and facilities, including control of fires from the air;

3. Physics and chemistry of combustion; and

4. Other matters involved in promoting greater efficiency in the prevention and control of forest fires and reducing costs and losses (Watts 1949).

As the Mann Gulch fire demonstrated, greater understanding of the fundamentals of fire and fire behavior was needed to improve fire management of America's wildlands. It also showed how this knowledge could save firefighters' lives. So in spite of reduced budgets and declining support for research during the early 1950s, particularly at the smaller western facilities, fire research continued at Priest River in three areas: fire behavior, fire danger rating, and fire control.

Like Jack Barrows, forester C.E. (Mike) Hardy joined the Forest Service on a permanent basis after WWII but then took time off to pursue a graduate degree. When Hardy returned from Michigan in the spring of 1949 with a Master's degree in forest management, he was soon assigned to the fire danger rating system. It was meant to be a 2-year program, Hardy recalled, developing more weather stations and continuing the work of Harry Gisborne. As part of his assignment, Hardy visited every ranger station in the region and talked to fire lookouts by telephone, helping explain how to take accurate weather readings and how the numbers they gathered were used for rating fire danger in the region (C. E. Hardy, personal communication 2010).

At the same time, even though funding for research continued to be tight throughout the Forest Service, in 1952 Congress appropriated additional funds to help fight fires.

With new funding, the Forest Service was authorized to build a dormitory, parachute loft, and warehouse for a new smokejumper center in Missoula, Montana, replacing the early training center at Seeley Lake Ranger Station, the Ninemile airfield, and the old Missoula airport that was then south of town. This new smokejumper center broke ground in an area west of Missoula, next to the new airport. While this particular facility was dedicated to mobilizing a quick response to wildland fires, it initiated a new Forest Service complex that would, a few years later, become home to the Fire Lab (McArdle 1953).

In 1953, the USDA announced another series of significant changes, including the reorganization and mergers of the Northern Rocky Mountain Research Station in Missoula with the Intermountain Forest and Range Experiment Station in Ogden. One of the first decisions managers had to make was where to locate Station headquarters. According to Laurence Lassen, former Director of the Intermountain Research Station, the decision fell to Reed Bailey, who was director in Ogden at the time. Bailey was nearing retirement and not in the best of health. He had been scheduled to transfer to Berkeley to head the California Forest and Range Experiment Station but had decided not to go. He also did not want to move to Missoula. Therefore, Bailey announced that headquarters would remain in Ogden, keeping Missoula as a field office (Lassen 2009). With the new organization in place and limited funding available for research, fire-related research at Priest River and the winter headquarters in the Federal building in Missoula might have inched along without much support, but Jack Barrows kept pushing for support for new research and a new facility for conducting it.

While Bailey did not want to relocate to Missoula, he still agreed to travel with Jack Barrows in March 1957 to Washington, DC, to meet with Montana Representative Lee Metcalf and convince him that a centralized fire research lab was needed. According to Hardy, Barrows also enlisted the Missoula Chamber of Commerce to lobby on the proposed project's behalf (C. E. Hardy, personal communication 2010). They must have made a convincing argument because on July 8, 1957, Montana Senators Mike Mansfield and James Murray introduced Senate Bill 2596 to authorize the Secretary of Agriculture to conduct a comprehensive program of forest-fire research. House Resolution 8852 was introduced by Lee Metcalf on July 22, 1957. Both houses of Congress considered the bills, but the outcome seemed uncertain until the Russian launch of Sputnik helped influence the decision about this proposed $1 million facility in Missoula, Montana.

Seeding Clouds to Prevent Lightning-Caused Fires

New knowledge, techniques, and equipment are being developed for the suppression and possibly for the prevention of lightning fires. This is a very important research program for the West. In the Rocky Mountain States, some 70 percent of the forest fires are caused by lightning. The research program in this field, known as Project Skyfire, offers exciting possibilities for improved forest protection over a vast area in the West and interior Alaska (Metcalf 1958).

Lightning starts thousands of wildfires each year in the Rocky Mountain West, costing millions of dollars to fight. In addition, these lightning-caused fires often occur at elevations of 7,000 feet (or more) above sea level, where limited access can hamper fire suppression. Clearly, if researchers could better understand the causes of lightning-caused fires and either find a way to prevent lightning strikes or defuse lightning-causing storms, this could reduce significantly one of the West's major causes of fires. So when Harry Gisborne first learned of Vincent Schaefer's research at General Electric using dry ice to seed clouds, he immediately started investigating whether or not this technique could be used to control lightning-caused fires.

In early February 1948, Gisborne visited Schaefer at his General Electric offices in Schenectady, New York, and invited Schaefer and his family to visit him at Priest River. That summer, Schaefer and his family drove out to Idaho where "Schaefer, Gisborne, and [Jack] Barrows spent considerable time together ... recording lightning, taking lapse-time movies of cloud life cycles, and discussing the theories of mountain thunderstorms and means of subduing them" (Hardy 1977). The three men also considered and discussed different hypotheses about the exact processes that might produce lightning storms.

Don Fuquay, Vincent Schaefer, and Jack Barrows (left to right) in 1956, working on Project Skyfire (photo: USDA Forest Service).

As Schaefer recalled, based on their observations and discussions that summer, it appeared that when a large cumulus formed on the western side of a ridge it would "glaciate," forming ice crystals that would be "blown from the west towards the storms forming over the ridge of the mountains." The three researchers believed that when the storm clouds were "seeded" by the ice crystals, big thunderstorms would develop. The discussions among Schaefer, Gisborne, and Barrows at Priest River "planted the seed in [Shaefer's] mind for the development of the full blown research endeavor that became Project Skyfire,"[1] officially launched in 1953, and quickly became one of the cornerstones of Forest Service fire research. "We concluded that perhaps it would be possible to change the pattern of glaciations by early seeding operations. If this could be done we might change the nature of the charge development pattern" (Schaefer and Hardy 1976).

Following in Gisborne and Hardy's footsteps, one of the project's first actions was to organize those already working in fire detection to gather data. A network of fire lookout stations was established, with observers trained in specific aspects of meteorology. In 1952, Irving Langmuir from General Electric came to Missoula to help organize a training school "to keep track of lightning storms through the Northern Rocky area and to make cloud surveys of the area" (Barrows 1976). Lookouts learned to record when and where thunderstorms occurred, how long they lasted, and how much lightning they produced, providing a rich database that researchers could compare with fire activity in the region (Arnold 1964).

After preliminary investigations, the project conducted cloud-seeding experiments in Northern Arizona and Montana starting in 1956. These experiments "provided some of the basic information for the design of more comprehensive experiments," according to Jack Barrows, who co-directed the research with Schaefer after Gisborne's death. In the summer of 1957, a network of cloud-seeding generators was placed along the summit of the Bitterroot Range in the Lolo National Forest, and on 24 of the 29 days the generators were operated, the researchers detected cloud modification in the form of ice crystals, which could impact the cloud's electrical activity. Barrows and his colleagues also adapted surplus military radar to detect, track, and analyze lightning storms in the region (Barrows 1958).

As the program developed, it became clear to researchers that "basic information was needed before experiments in cloud seeding could be designed or the results understood." Thus, Project Skyfire expanded to include several partners, including the U.S. Weather Bureau, Montana State University (now the University of Montana), the University of Washington, California State Division of Forestry, and the National Park Service. The scope of the research also broadened to include literature reviews of other cloud-seeding experiments and analyses of both thunderstorms and lightning fire occurrence in the Northern Rockies (Barrows and others 1958).

Launching a National Commitment to Science and Research

In the era already referred to as the space age, we too must make our mark (Barrows 1958).

When the Russian government sent Sputnik I into space in October 1957, it also helped launch a new era of science education and research in America. And while forestry research wasn't considered a high national priority at that time, historians now consider the period of the late 1950s into the 1970s as the "Golden Era" of Forest Service research, resulting in the growth of research programs, laboratory construction, equipment purchases, increased staffing, and operating money (Lassen 2009). The bills to establish what was then called the Northern Forest Fire Laboratory were introduced before the Sputnik launch so they cannot be viewed as a direct response to that historic event. However, the actual appropriation, months after Sputnik made international news, surely benefited in part from the push to restore America's technological preeminence in the world. With bi-partisan support, Congress appropriated the necessary funds in 1958 (Klade 2006).

Senator Mike Mansfield, one of the bill's co-sponsors, presented a compelling view of the comprehensive research program to be conducted at the lab. According to Mansfield, the new Northern Forest Fire Laboratory would investigate (1) factors controlling the start and behavior of fires and their interrelations; (2) atmospheric factors that lead to fire-causing lightning storms, and potential ways to prevent or modify the storms; (3) factors that cause some fires to "blow up" and defy efforts of control; (4) improved fire control systems, methods and practices; and (5) effective use of fire in land management (Mansfield 1958).

Harry Gisborne, Jack Barrows, and C.E. (Mike) Hardy had already initiated many of these programs from their offices in the Missoula Federal Building and their field research site at Priest River. But as Mansfield explained, researchers lacked the state-of-the-art equipment, facilities, and personnel to pursue these research projects in depth. The new Fire Lab would allow researchers to investigate these areas in much greater detail. And, in tune with the political climate of the time, he added an extra incentive:

---

[1]An audio interview with Jack Barrows from October 21, 1951, about Project Skyfire is available at http://archives.cbc.ca/science_technology/natural_science/topics/849-4927/.

Lightning is one of the major causes of fire in the Rocky Mountain West (photo: Fire Science Digest [BLM]).

Northern Forest Fire Research Laboratory, Missoula, Montana, 1961 (*photo: USDA Forest Service*).

Recent discussions over the hydrogen bomb have focused attention on the importance of weather control. The program of the Missoula fire research group is a perfect example of the very things being stressed. Here is a program in being, already producing promising leads in a vital field.... They are operating on a shoestring. With a little more support, I believe that they will make great contributions to forest protection and to an important field of science (Mansfield 1958).

On December 9, 1958, Jack Barrows gave a talk on "fire fighting in laboratories" to the Western Forest Fire Research Council meeting in San Francisco where he laid out his vision for the new facility. "New knowledge is the foundation for the progress of our civilization" he said, and "future progress in the protection and management of western forests rests heavily upon research." Barrows showed slides of a 20,000-acre human-caused fire, marked by intense heat, high flammability, and fire in surface fuels

and in the tree crowns. Barrows used these photos as a backdrop to illustrate what drove the kinds of questions researchers wanted to answer in the new facility. For example, is it possible to predict the behavior of such a fire, or better yet, to prevent it? Once such a fire is underway, what are the best mechanical or chemical methods to suppress it? (Barrows 1958a).

For the Forest Service and other agencies to be able to predict, prevent, and suppress wildfires, they must thoroughly understand the nature of fire, Barrows explained. As Gisborne had argued before him, researchers must have the ability to isolate individual factors like temperature, humidity, and wind, as well as the type of fuel, and study them under controlled conditions. It also became clear that in order to develop and test electronic methods to detect lightning fires, use radar to track lightning storms, and create new equipment and techniques to prevent lightning through cloud seeding, the project needed access to better research facilities. As both Senator Mansfield and Representative Lee Metcalf argued on behalf of the proposed Fire Lab, it cost the nation literally millions of dollars to suppress wildland fires. The $1 million requested to build a state-of-the-art fire research facility in Missoula, if it provided the research needed to suppress even one major forest fire, would more than pay for itself. The new Northern Forest Fire Laboratory would soon provide researchers with just the kinds of facilities that both Gisborne and Barrows had envisioned.

Section II: Missoula Fire Lab History

Fire fighter photo by Jeff Henry, National Parks Service; all others USDA Forest Service.

Fire Science: A New Beginning

Protecting forests from fire requires marshalling of the full technical resources of the nation. These technical resources must stem primarily from a creative fire research program that feeds knowledge, ideas, and techniques to the fire fighting agencies. The Northern Forest Fire Laboratory has been designed and built, and will be staffed for this express purpose (USDA Forest Service 1960).

With several successful fire research programs already underway in Missoula, and with the full support of the Montana Congressional delegation, funding for the Northern Forest Fire Research facility was secured through bipartisan support in Congress in 1958. The Montana facility was the second of three fire-related research facilities that eventually would be supported by the Forest Service: the Southern Forest Fire Laboratory, in Macon, Georgia, established in 1959; the Northern Forest Fire Laboratory, in Missoula, opened in 1960; and the Forest Fire Laboratory in Riverside, California, dedicated in 1963. The Missoula lab had two broad goals: (1) to perform basic and applied research on critical wildland fire problems having nationwide application; and (2) to conduct regional research on fire problems peculiar to the Intermountain West and Alaska.

The new research facilities dedicated in Missoula on September 12, 1960, included a combustion laboratory where researchers could control air temperature, atmospheric pressure, and relative humidity and, thus, compare rate of spread under various conditions. Two wind tunnels allowed researchers to control another variable crucial to understanding fire spread, while the new fuels laboratory enabled researchers to measure and analyze fire conditions based on the condition of the fuel itself (for example, leaves, needles, grass, bark, tree limbs, twigs, etc.). Other new facilities included a physics and chemistry laboratory; a meteorology laboratory for tracking weather and fire conditions; and a training room, where forest managers could watch research taking place in the combustion lab and learn about the science to help inform their decisions in the field (USDA Forest Service 1960). Thus, with these new facilities, researchers could investigate the causes and behavior of wildland fires in new and creative ways while evaluating different variables such as moisture content or wind speed in controlled environments. By the time the Fire Lab was ready to open its doors, researchers were ready with several questions to pursue:

- Could new technology, such as radar, electronic warning systems, or heat-sensing devices, rapidly and accurately detect fires?
- What conditions resulted in small fires becoming big ones, and how do you measure the effects of weather,

Jack Barrows in the new Northern Forest Fire Research Laboratory, c. 1960 (*photo: USDA Forest Service*).

fuels, and topography on fire?
- Is it possible to "fire proof" wildland areas prone to fire or develop fire hazard-reduction techniques?
- Once firefighters were on the ground, could research make their job easier and safer through new fire suppression techniques and/or the development of new chemical agents?
- Could safer or more effective burning techniques be developed for burning logging slash, removing unwanted vegetation, or using fire to prepare seed beds? (USDA Forest Service 1960)?

Before these research questions could be addressed, however, Jack Barrows needed to fully staff the new facility.

Taking an Interdisciplinary Approach

Before the Lab was dedicated, the employment roster showed 15 regular personnel in fire research, including clerical staff. Only three scientific disciplines were represented. This was not the type of staffing Lab Chief Jack Barrows needed if the organization was to develop a fire research program that would be [in Barrows' own words] 'helping to bring the full strength of modern science to American forests' (Klade 2006).

In 1961, the Fire Lab's first full year of operation, the facility still lacked the personnel necessary to pursue rigorous, multi-disciplinary fire research in earnest. Jack Barrows and C.E. (Mike) Hardy, for example, were both foresters. Barrows recognized that increased understanding of the basics of fire behavior would require input from physical scientists and engineers (Wells 2008), so he looked to the Idaho National Engineering Laboratory (INEL) in Idaho Falls, operated by General Electric, where a number of scientists and engineers were about to be laid off after the cancelation of a nuclear airplane program. Although nuclear power and aircraft development might seem far afield for a fire research center, many of the researchers working at INEL had the science and engineering skills that Barrows and other foresters lacked.

At INEL, Barrows met and later hired physicist Hal Anderson, electrical engineer Stanley (Stan) Hirsch, and aeronautical engineer Richard (Dick) Rothermel, all of whom would soon become leaders at the fledgling research lab (Klade 2006). He also hired two skilled INEL electronic technicians: Erwin (Erv) Breuer and Merlin Brown. By the end of 1961, most of the first generation of researchers had been hired and were starting to work in earnest at the new facility, exploring its capabilities and designing tests to further knowledge in several areas of fire research.

Wildland fire managers have always understood that many factors need to be considered when making fire-fighting decisions, and Barrows knew that they usually responded based on personal experience and judgment. The new facility offered researchers the opportunity to quantify some of these factors, helping field staff supplement their personal judgment with science to make more informed decisions, including how to allocate resources. But this was a new facility, with no established protocols to follow, so exactly what could be accomplished was not clear. As Richard Rothermel recalled, researchers debated two different approaches: "bring in box-car loads of fuel from all over the country for burning in the wind tunnels," or "weld the doors shut until a logical plan for use of the facilities was developed." In the end, they followed a middle ground, calibrating and experimenting with the equipment while working to understand fire spread in fuels and adapting concepts of modeling and systems to the problems of forest fire prediction (Rothermel 1983).

For example, researchers wanted to know what happens when the moisture content of grasses or debris drops below a certain level. Do these conditions necessarily result in the risk of a catastrophic fire? If so, how can forest managers decide when to exercise extreme caution when managing a fire in their region? As Edward Cliff, Chief of the Forest Service, noted in his 1961 annual report, early research at the Fire Lab focused on these and similar questions, while the scientists pursued "a better method of predicting the rate of spread of forest fires from measurements on model fires" (Cliff 1962).

By the end of 1962, lab experiments designed by Hal Anderson and Richard Rothermel had tested fire behavior using a full range of moisture content of fuels, and produced new insights into fire rate of spread and intensity. According to Chief Cliff, this early Fire Lab research suggested that flammability increases slowly until fuel moisture content decreases to about 6 percent. "As moisture decreases below this point, however, flammability increases more and more abruptly, approaching a virtually explosive burning condition."

This insight might appear to be an insignificant bit of information to add to overall understanding about fire behavior, but it directly impacted how wildland fire managers and others assessed fire danger under different field conditions. It had, according to Cliff, "immediate application in field practice, red-flagging those occasional days when the moisture in [fine] forest fuels drops to 5 percent or below" (Cliff 1963). Thus, piece by piece, the new cadre of researchers at the Northern Forest Fire Laboratory added to the nation's understanding of the fundamentals of combustion and wildland fire behavior, building on the commitment to research and "management by science" philosophy of Gifford Pinchot and the applied research approach developed by Harry Gisborne.

As research continued at the Fire Lab, fundamental knowledge about fire behavior accumulated very quickly. But managers in the field still needed what Richard Rothermel later referred to as "a consistent method for predicting fire spread and intensity in these fuels" (Rothermel 1972). Thus, researchers faced an on-going challenge to transform the volumes of data they were accumulating into a systematic form that field managers could use to make informed decisions quickly and accurately.

Laying the Groundwork

When Hal Anderson and I came to the [N]orthern Forest Fire Laboratory in 1961, it was not yet a year old and there was a feeling that surely it was going to contribute. Just what would be accomplished was not entirely clear, but things were going to happen. There was also a sense of being overwhelmed, not only by all the unknowns of wildfire behavior, but also by how to use this brand new facility (Rothermel 1983).

The initial task was to prepare the new equipment to do fire experiments. The wind created in the big wind tunnel, for example, was quite turbulent, so Richard Rothermel and his colleagues experimented with adding layers of window screen in the mouth of the tunnel to smooth the flow of air. In the combustion lab, Hal Anderson figured out how to weigh the fuel bed as it was burning to measure the energy release rate—a variable not previously measured successfully. The scientists also set up a moisture chamber to precondition the fuel and radiometers to measure heat transfer. They measured rate of fire spread, and used thermocouples to measure air temperature. In essence, the researchers were learning how to measure variables and conduct fire experiments in these new facilities, and the results were impressive.

Physicist Hal Anderson in 1962 at the Fire Lab's control center. One of the early challenges facing the first generation of researchers was learning how to effectively use all the new equipment to conduct fire experiments (*photo: USDA Forest Service*).

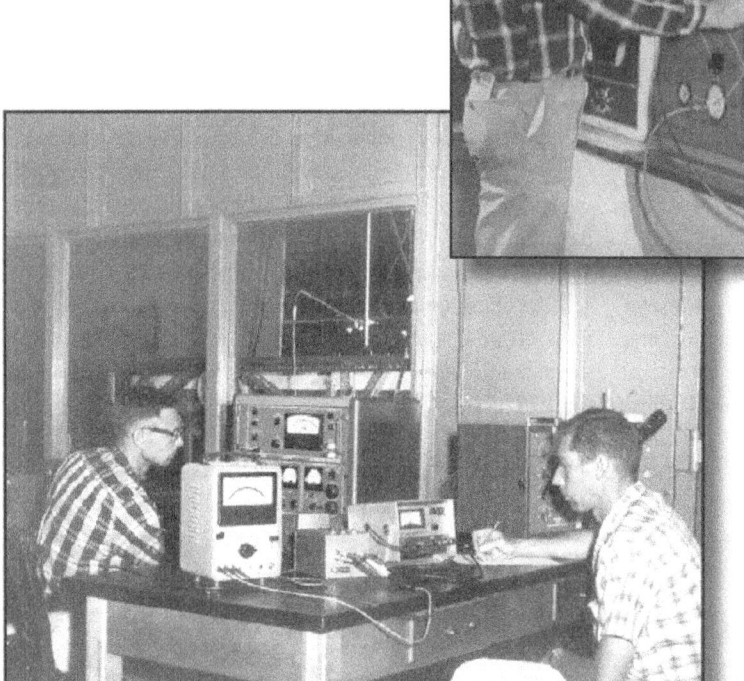

Richard (Dick) Rothermel (left) and Merlin Brown take measurements of air conditions in the large wind tunnel at the Fire Lab, 1963 (*photo: USDA Forest Service*).

In 1965, just 5 years after the lab opened and only 4 years after they were hired, Anderson and Rothermel presented a paper at the International Symposium of the Combustion Institute, in Cambridge, England. In it they documented the differing effects of environmental conditions on the characteristics of approximately 200 fires burned under controlled humidity, air velocity, and fuel moisture.

While their work was empirically based in these early years, it also laid the foundation for the more conceptual approach that researchers knew would eventually be needed: the characterization of all fires by combustion rate and rate of spread with a "general equation that predicts rate of spread in any wood fuel ... by incorporating fuel particle size and fuel bed compactness with fuel moisture content and air velocity." Rothermel's fire model was already in its formative stages (Anderson and Rothermel 1965).

Fire Danger and Fire Behavior

Even though there are some holes in our information, we have much more than our predecessors. Those men had to think of EVERYTHING.... But times have changed... While we might like to have more, I doubt that anyone ever will be able to sit down to a machine, punch a key for every factor of the situation, and have the machine tell him what to do. Fire control still requires headwork based on knowledge. If we will make a purposeful attempt to use all of the knowledge and all of the facilities that are available to us today we can do one thing the old timers could not do: We can come mighty close to getting adequate fire control, and at an operating cost far below what it used to be (Gisborne 1948).

Harry Gisborne developed his first fire danger meter in 1931 with the goal of eventually developing a fire danger rating system that could be applied throughout the country. Indeed, as word of Gisborne's meter spread, it was put into use across the United States. However, foresters modified the meter to include what they considered to be their own region's specific needs. For example, in the Southeast, the sticks used to gauge fuel moisture were replaced by Venetian blind material—"Appalachian slats"—to represent the Southeast's abundance of fine fuels. While adaptations to reflect local conditions increased local adoption of Gisborne's technology, they also diminished Gisborne's ultimate goal of developing a "common language" for fire danger rating. At the 1958 national meeting of the American Meteorological Society, as three national fire labs were under development, C.E. (Mike) Hardy asked whether or not it was possible to develop a uniform fire danger rating system and put it into practice throughout the United States (Hardy 1958).

In 1964, the Forest Service transferred Jack Barrows to Washington to head the agency's national fire research program. Now he was in a position to build Harry Gisborne's fire danger rating system—which had become fragmented and localized—into a consistent national application. Once in Washington, Barrows assembled a research team at each of the nation's fire laboratories—Missoula, Montana; Macon, Georgia; and Riverside, California—to develop it, and assigned John Deeming to lead a team headquartered in Fort Collins, Colorado, to integrate results from the three fire labs and implement a National Fire Danger Rating System. Having seen the kind of research that could be done in the lab's wind tunnel, Barrows initially assigned the Missoula researchers the task of characterizing the effect of wind on fire behavior. But, as Richard Rothermel recalled, it quickly became clear that "you cannot separate the effect of wind, the effect of moisture, the effect of fuel particle size, fuel loading, the slope—all of these things interact."

Based on the success of their earlier work characterizing the effects of fuel moisture on fire behavior, Rothermel and physicists Hal Anderson and Bill Frandsen turned their attention to characterizing fire behavior generally, initiating a series of experiments. Rothermel began to describe the results in a mathematical model that included all of these effects. The model (published in 1972) was initially developed to serve as the foundation for a new, nationally relevant fire danger rating system as requested by Barrows, and it was integrated successfully into that effort (Rothermel, personal communication 2010). But the fire model soon took on a life of its own.

Engineering a Way to Predict the Behavior of Fire

Rothermel and his team completed development of the model in a hurry, in response to their superiors' demands for a way to reliably predict fire danger over broad landscapes. What it lacks in complexity, it makes up in reliability and ease of use. Even today, despite widely acknowledged limitations—which Rothermel is the first to point out—the Rothermel model of fire spread and intensity is still the most widely used, and it is a component of many fire management tools now in use (Wells 2008).

Richard Rothermel approached the challenge of defining fire danger as an engineering problem, with the idea of finding a quantitative way to describe the essentials of "the fuels, the weather, the topography, and something about the fire." By using the burn chamber and wind tunnels to isolate the effects of factors such as wind, temperature, humidity, slope, and density and porosity of fuel, researchers could reduce "the number of trials required and the time needed to analyze the results of each" (Cliff 1967). The goal was to put these variables into a mathematical model that could be used to predict fire intensity, rate of spread, and flame length.

The resulting model reduces wildland fire to "a set of equations operating in a hypothetical universe in which fires burn only small, uniform, dead fuels on the forest floor" (Wells 2008). The Rothermel model does not distinguish between lodgepole pine and redwood stands, for example—specific fuel models would be developed separately. Instead, it describes the physical and chemical processes of fire in fundamental terms assuming very basic fuels, based in part on fundamental research by Forest Service chemists Ronald Susott and Charles Philpot, and fire scientist Robert Mutch.

Rothermel's model, published in 1972 as *A Mathematical Model for Predicting Fire Spread in Wildland Fuels*, is still cited as one of the groundbreaking works in understanding fire behavior and the spread of wildland fires (Klade 2006). As Rothermel wrote in his introduction, the model offered "for the first time a method for making quantitative evaluations of both rate of spread and fire intensity in fuels that qualify for the assumptions made on the model. Fuel and weather parameters *measurable in the field* are featured as inputs to the model" (Rothermel 1972).

While this model was only the first of many methods developed to predict the behavior of fire in the field, Rothermel and his colleagues understood that it was a giant step toward providing the knowledge that might result in a forest manager being able to "sit down to a machine [and] punch a key for every factor of the situation" as described in 1948 by Harry Gisborne. And yet, even this significant advance

Fire Lab combustion chamber, photographed in the mid-1960s (*photo: USDA Forest Service*).

in fundamental understanding of fire behavior would not be of much use if fire managers did not understand the model or, more to the point, could not apply it when making their decisions.

Rothermel completed the fire behavior model before the introduction of personal computers. How could wildland managers use such a sophisticated mathematical model to make informed decisions quickly and accurately? In 1973, mechanical engineer Frank Albini joined the Fire Lab and, according to Rothermel, "let the genie out of the bottle with publication of his book of nomograms" (Rothermel 1983).

Making Mathematics More User Friendly

As the base of knowledge grows, new puzzles will emerge, and explanations that were once accepted will be challenged as their implications are explored. But useful results have been produced from the present level of understanding, and continued research should yield substantial rewards in terms of safer, more economical control and use of wildland fire (Albini 1984).

During his 12-year career at the Fire Lab, Frank Albini worked on a number of analytical and experimental research projects, investigating the basic processes governing the behavior of wildland fires. His research was highly diverse and ranged from investigating the intricacies of flame structure to predicting crown fire spread. But it was Albini's publication of a series of graphs, or "nomograms" as they were

called, that made application of the Fire Lab's sophisticated modeling capability feasible for managers to use in the field to predict fire spread (Albini 1976).

Based on Richard Rothermel's fire spread model, Albini's nomograms consisted of a set of visual calculating devices that could be used in real time to estimate fire spread, intensity, flame length, and difficulty of control. Rather than requiring managers to deal with abstract concepts and complex calculations, the nomograms allowed them, whether in the office or the field, to read fire spread rate and intensity almost as easily as they might read a map. This approach proved to be so successful that it continued to be used as a training aid and field tool even after the introduction of computer programs that would make exact calculations of fire behavior characteristics (Andrews 2006).

The nomograms also allowed researchers to teach concepts about fire behavior in new ways to forest and fire managers. Rothermel had been an early and strong proponent of technology transfer and education. Albini's nomograms took the ability to transfer use of Rothermel's model to a new level because the models could be introduced visually. The nomograms illustrated the relationships between variables and, according to Patricia Andrews, "allowed for a quick estimation of spread rate, flame length, and intensity based on a minimum of information" (Andrews 1986).

The same year Albini published his nomograms, the director of Forest Service training, Ernie Anderson, asked a team from the Fire Lab, including Rothermel, to develop a 2-week training course at Marana, Arizona, to teach fire managers how to use the fire spread model in the field. In response to Anderson's request, Fire Lab scientists took the

Frank Albini, 1984. Albini created visual calculating devices ("nomograms") that allowed field personnel to estimate fire spread, intensity, flame length and difficulty of control. His nomograms were also used for teaching concepts about fire behavior (*photo: USDA Forest Service*).

lead in developing and teaching the course to analysts with responsibility for fire suppression (Rothermel 1983).

As Rothermel recalled, participants in the early training courses at Marana were encouraging and the classes were a success. Indeed, in 1981, the Forest Service formally recognized Rothermel's contributions to both fire research and education, awarding him the prestigious USDA Superior Service Award for "outstanding creativity in developing fire behavior prediction technology and training programs, enhancing the implementation of the Forest Service's revised fire policy."

In 1983, Rothermel published a handbook, *How to Predict the Spread and Intensity of Forest and Range Fires*, based on material presented at the Marana training center. It included a guide for using the new TI-59, a handheld calculator equipped with a pre-programmed chip to run the model, developed by Robert (Bob) Burgan in 1979 (Rothermel 1983). By 1986, fire behavior and fire danger rating models were made available on the more advanced HP-71b handheld calculator (Klade 2006).

While Fire Lab researchers continued to develop a fundamental understanding of the nature of fire and fire behavior, they concurrently looked for new technologies and other methods to distill and synthesize that understanding into forms that could be used to make decisions in the field. This was a relatively new focus for Forest Service researchers. As Rothermel noted, the Forest Service had done research for years but researchers normally "shunned"

Patricia (Pat) Andrews introduces Frank Albini's nomograms at the 1974 Tall Timbers Fire Ecology Conference in Missoula (*photo: USDA Forest Service*).

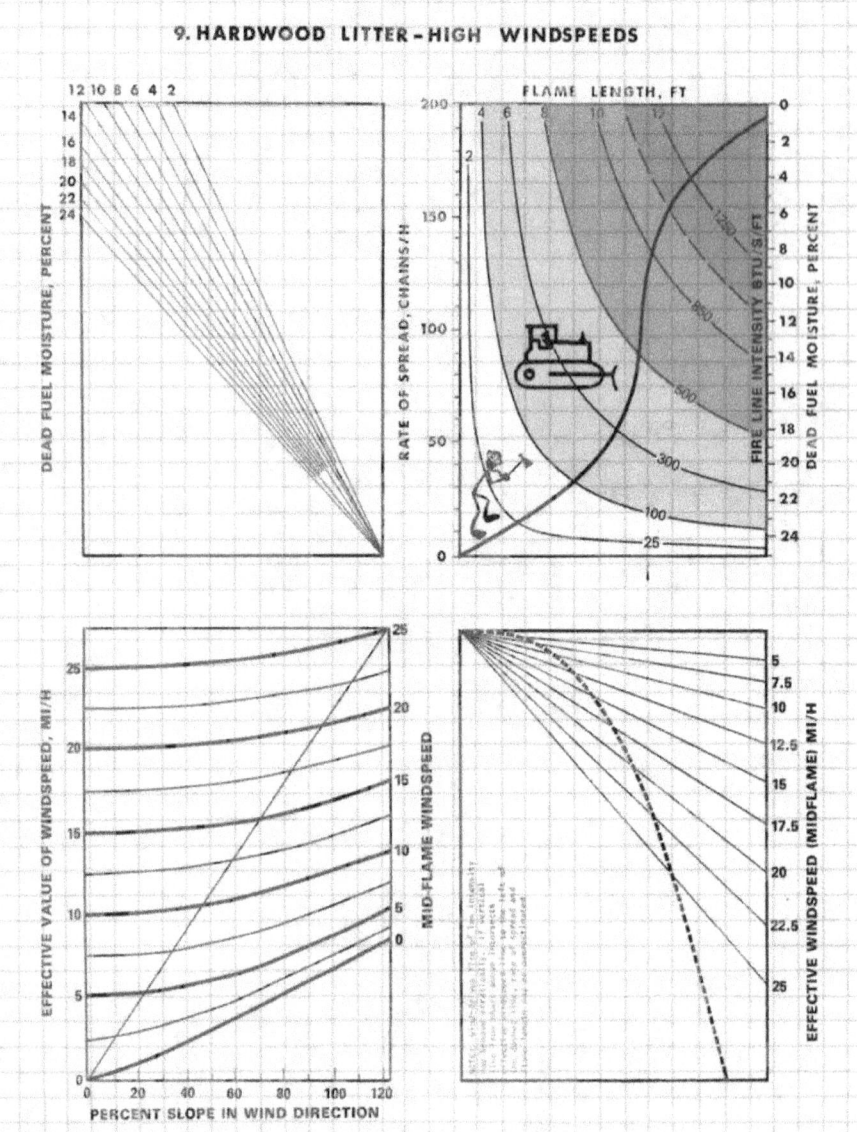

An example of Frank Albini's nomographs or "nomograms" as they were called, a group of interconnecting graphs used for estimating a fire's rate of spread, fireline intensity, flame length, and heat output. Albini developed two nomograms (high wind and low wind) for each of the 13 fuel models associated with Rothermel's fire model. By entering maximum slope, wind speed, and fuel moisture variables onto the graphs, managers can visually calculate fire behavior and make informed, real-time decisions about responding to the fire (*photo: USDA Forest Service*).

technology transfer (Rothermel 1983). But researchers at the Fire Lab made an early commitment to transferring fire-related research and new technologies. As this new research was ready for field application, it led to new training needs and resulted in new training materials and courses.

Transferring New Knowledge to the Field

The people who take the training usually come in with fire experience, so they can use the models to make good decisions. Computers have gotten so much better and the outputs look so pretty and final, it's a concern to a lot of us that people sometimes believe them too much. Trust in the program outputs is particularly true for planners, who may not have

the experience that fire behavior analysts have, but they still have to make decisions, and want to use these tools to make their decisions (Andrews 2010).

With an advanced degree in mathematics and training in computers, Patricia (Pat) Andrews started at the Fire Lab as a programmer in 1973, working with physicist Bill Frandsen. The Rothermel fire spread model assumes uniform and continuous fuels, so Frandsen developed a way to apply the Rothermel model to non-uniform fuels, which Andrews programmed. Frandsen's idea was ahead of its time, according to Andrews, limited only by available computer technology.

Patricia (Pat) Andrews at a Fire Behavior Analyst training course in 1983 at Marana, Arizona (*photo: USDA Forest Service*).

When Andrews began to program computer-based systems that integrated a number of Fire Lab models, she also began teaching at Marana to ensure that fire managers and planners could successfully apply them. As she explained, training has been an important part of the Fire Lab's history because it provides an excellent venue to get new research into application. Training also allows knowledge to flow from fire managers to researchers as these scientists have opportunities to talk to the people in the field and learn what they need. In 1994, her contributions to training and systems development were recognized by the Forest Service, which presented her with the Superior Science Award.

Calculating New Applications

We were able to predict behavior at the [Kootenai Forest] fire in a couple of minutes... Without it, we would have taken a couple of hours to do it manually, or we would have gone back to the station to use the computer (Bailey 1979).

In 1973, Bill Frandsen published his work on Rothermel's fire spread model programmed for the Hewlett-Packard 9820, "one of the early programs that made it possible to use the fire spread model with a programmable calculator." In 1979, building on this work, forester Robert (Bob) Burgan developed a program for use with a hand-held Texas Instrument model-59 (TI-59) calculator (Burgan

1979). With a small calculator in hand, managers now had a machine they could take into the field that could both save time and increase precision over the manual methods of the nomograms.

As Burgan and colleague Jack Cohen explained in announcing the launch of the program's capabilities, the calculator's "high portability, procedural convenience, and time savings" allowed fire managers to make faster and more accurate fire behavior estimates in fire camp and on fire reconnaissance. In addition, the TI-59 program allowed users to simultaneously enter information on two different fuels "to calculate the combined rate of spread." By streamlining and simplifying the process, the Texas Instrument calculator could also be used for "on-site quantitative fire analysis for such activities as prescribed burning, management fires, and escaped fire analysis" (Cohen and Burgan 1978).

Greening up the Fire Danger Rating System

Starting in 1988, I went from watching fires burn at less than a centimeter an hour to working with remote sensing which covered kilometers on the ground. I went from fundamental scientific observations to watching vegetation change using satellite remote sensing, which allows for a lot of artistic and intuitive interpretation (Bartlette 2010).

Robert (Bob) Burgan (on right) with Richard Rothermel and Patricia Andrews at a "BEHAVE in the Wilderness!" symposium and workshop on wilderness fire, held in Missoula, Montana 1985 (*photo: USDA Forest Service*).

In 1968, forester Roberta (Bobbie) Bartlette worked part time at the Fire Lab as a technician. She was only 18. When funding for her appointment ran out and she graduated from college, she worked as a fire lookout, led a Forest Service crew inventorying surface fuels, and taught high school science, before returning to work at the Fire Lab fulltime as a technician in 1976.

In 1981, Bartlette and physicist Ralph Wilson worked on a field study of West Texas grasses and other fuels. On that research trip, Texas Tech graduate students encouraged Bartlette to pursue a graduate degree based on the work she was doing. She soon entered the master's program in the University of Montana's School of Forestry, with a

focus on fire science. As part of her studies, Bartlette began investigating research creating a greenness index and determining the relationship of vegetation greenness to fire danger, a problem that Bob Burgan was also working on. For her graduate research, Bartlette established field plots to determine how vegetation greenness and the moisture content in these test grasslands changed through the season, could be monitored using satellite imagery, and could then be used to improve fire behavior predictions.

Burgan and Bartlette developed greenness ratings using satellite imagery and maps for the National Fire Danger Rating System. As the technology improved, they created entire color-coded maps of fire danger in the United States, which they made available on the Internet. To help managers use this new approach to understanding fire danger, Bartlette joined Patricia Andrews as one of the few women teaching at the Marana, Arizona, training center at the time.

Fueling Fire Models

Creating fuel models requires good science and good judgment. You input fuel characteristics into the fire model and see what it predicts. Then you do that for a lot of different vegetation types, which results in a blueprint of fire behavior by vegetation type. And then you have to make judgments. Is this realistic? Does the prediction for the grass confirm what your knowledge and research say are true? Then you do some fine tuning, adjusting the inputs to the model so that the fire behavior appears realistic relative to the other vegetation types (Brown 2010).

Roberta (Bobbie) Bartlette prepares fuel samples in 1969 for testing. Bartlette started part time at the Fire Lab in 1966 when she was still a student and eventually became a fulltime forester (*photo: USDA Forest Service*).

When estimating potential fire behavior, managers need to determine the type and characteristics of the fuel present. For example, grassland fuels burn differently than woody fuels, so those distinctions need to be made when determining fire behavior. According to Jim Brown, who developed some of the original fuel models used for calculating fire danger and predicting fire behavior, distinctions also exist within major fuel types; eastern grasslands, for instance, tend to have a lot more fuel than western grasslands, so behavior of grassland fires can be quite different in the two regions. The same is true of forest fuels, where different kinds of wood produce more or less heat, and burn faster or slower than others. Building on experience in the field and research in the lab, fuel modelers describe the physical characteristics and spatial distribution of grasses, brush, timber, and slash in mathematical terms; this quantitative description of fuel properties relevant to fire spread is known as a fuel model. Fuel models are needed as input for fire models, just as fuel itself is needed to feed a real fire (Brown, personal communication 2010).

The 1964 Fire Lab contributions to the National Fire Danger Rating System (NFDRS), for example, relied on fuel moisture, weather forecasts and two inputs for fuel types—one for grasses and one for woody conditions. As part of the fire danger rating effort initiated by Barrows, Rothermel completed his fire behavior model in 1972. It had two main components: one on the intensity of fire and the other on the rate of spread. To calculate these values, it required a number of inputs including fuel load (or quantity), depth, particle size, moisture, and wind, which resulted in an estimate of fire behavior burning near the ground (i.e., not crown fires or large fuels) (Rothermel, personal communication 2010).

As research forester Jim Brown explained it, fuel models needed to relate to fuel characteristics recognizable by managers in the field (such as pine needle litter or shrubs), and depended on the experiences and insights of researchers to make them realistic representations of conditions on the ground (Brown, personal communication 2010). Brown helped develop a set of eleven fire behavior fuel models that were published with Rothermel's fire spread model in 1972. When Frank Albini developed his nomograms, he expanded the original set to thirteen fuel models. In 1982, Hal Anderson prepared a publication using photographs to describe these models for use in the field.

The fire danger rating team took Rothermel's 1972 fire model, which weighted fuels by surface area, and changed it to weight fuels by load (or quantity), thus, giving greater emphasis to larger fuels to reflect seasonal changes in fire danger. To this end, they developed a set of nine fire danger fuel models. When the National Fire Danger Rating System was updated in 1978, the number of fire danger fuel models grew to 20. (These 20 fuel models were unique to NFDRS and should not be confused with the 13 fuel models developed for fire behavior.)

Fuel assessment can also help managers in the field describe the amount of dead material on the forest floor and evaluate its fire hazard. Such information can be used to plan for fire prevention, fire suppression, and prescribed fires. Like Gisborne before them, Fire Lab scientists understood that the methods for assessing fuels must be easy to apply. In 1981, Bill Fischer addressed this problem by producing three handbooks with photographs to illustrate vegetation with a description of the fuel in terms of size

Example of a photo from one of William Fischer's three photo guides for appraising woody fuels in Montana, designed to help managers quickly assess downed fuel to plan fire management strategies including fire prevention and prescribed fire. The photo guides also included a fire potential rating with each photo (*photo: USDA Forest Service*).

distribution and quantity (Fischer 1981a,b,c). In particular, each fuel condition photographed included a "fire potential rating," one of the most important contributions of this series. Fischer's photo guides were the first of a series of publications that tied photos of fuel conditions (for example, trees, shrubs, grasses, etc.) to quantitative descriptions of their fuel properties and potential fire behavior.

Initially produced at the Fire Lab by Fischer, other photo-based field guides for fuels have since been produced by scientists nationally. For example, the Pacific Northwest Research Station has produced an entire series of stereo photo guides of fuel conditions throughout the United States. The more recent field guides by Fire Lab researcher Bob Keane and his team (Sikkink and others 2009) continue in this tradition.

Turning Models into Systems

It's important to clarify the difference between models and systems. A model is like Rothermel's fire spread model which consists of equations. There are also models for spotting distance and for fuel moisture. A system takes many mathematical models and puts them together into some kind of a package that fire managers can use. BehavePlus is the system I developed. It uses Rothermel's model and maybe 45 other models (Andrews 2010).

With the growth of knowledge about fire and fire behavior, and the development of so many different models characterizing these insights, managers in the field needed a way to use the models in an integrated form. New computer technology was becoming available to help scientists meet this need. Returning from a fire training session in Marana in 1976, Richard Rothermel suggested that Patricia Andrews create a system to automate Albini's nomograms and the tables taught in the Fire Behavior Officer course, and to include options that were too tedious to use with manual methods. Within a year, Andrews had the basics of the BEHAVE system in place and introduced it to her colleagues (Andrews, personal communication 2010).

Although designed specifically as an interactive system for practitioners, the initial BEHAVE system had to be run on a computer at the Lawrence Berkeley Lab in California. Thus, during its development, researchers at the Fire Lab could run the program, but it wasn't easily accessible to people in the field. By 1984, field access to more powerful computers had improved, so the system was officially transferred into use nationwide. As part of the technology transfer process, Andrews, Robert Burgan, and Richard Rothermel developed a BEHAVE course that they taught six times around the country, using a train-the-trainer approach (Andrews 2007).

BEHAVE quickly proved how valuable predictive tools developed by Fire Lab researchers could be to decision makers in the field. In the summer of 1984, fire managers used BEHAVE to predict the spread of a fire in the Gates of the Mountains Wilderness near Helena, Montana—the same area where the Mann Gulch fire had tragically surprised and killed 13 fire fighters. BEHAVE calculations indicated that further spread was unlikely under predicted weather conditions. Based on these projections, managers decided to use minimal suppression on the fire, saving hundreds of thousands of dollars. As Richard Klade noted in his history of the Intermountain Research Station, these savings more than paid for development of the program (Klade 2006). Since that time, better computers, better access to data (for example, fuel, weather, topography), and additional research models have led to new and improved systems. The redesigned BehavePlus fire modeling system replaced BEHAVE in 2001, and Version 5 of BehavePlus was released in 2010 (http://www.firemodels.org/index.php/behaveplussoftware/behaveplus-downloads).

New technology facilitated research innovation again in 1993, when research forester Mark Finney, a Fire Lab contractor at the time, developed the FARSITE fire area simulator. FARSITE uses the improved graphical capabilities of computers to model and display fire growth across the landscape under changing weather conditions. The system can be used to predict the growth of on-going fires and assist with planning (for example, to explore "what-if" questions). In keeping with the Fire Lab's technology transfer tradition, once FARSITE was available for widespread release, Finney and others developed a course for the NWCG fire behavior training program. Finney continues to develop more advanced fire modeling systems, including Fire Spread Probability (FSPro), a program used to support decision making on large, complex fires, and the Wildland Fire Decision Support System (WFDSS). This system integrates multiple Fire Lab models into an easy-to-use, more intuitive, and responsive system to assist fire managers and analysts in making strategic and tactical decisions for fire incidents. Its web-based application makes it easier for fire managers to document their decision-making process, and share analyses and reports with other fire managers. In another key advance, it introduces economic principles into the fire-decision process.

Since the late 1970s, researchers at the Fire Lab have made models available in systems for all aspects of wildland fire management (for example, prescribed fire planning, fire suppression, budget planning). Models of fire behavior, fire effects, and ecosystem dynamics are packaged into systems that can help researchers and practitioners visualize changes in vegetation over hundreds of years. This kind of modeling can play an important role in studying relationships between wildland fire and climate change.

[T]he fire problem on national forests is probably not for solution by the Forest Service alone …. THE MAJOR NEED AND OPPORTUNITY is for a new, truly national concept followed by coordination of effort by many agencies (Gisborne 1941).

As Jack Barrows recognized when hiring Fire Lab personnel, to be successful wildfire research requires the skills and talents of many different people with diverse backgrounds and expertise. This commitment to collaboration and working with those who can bring a unique perspective to the research question continues to this day. For example, for more than 30 years, researchers at the Fire Lab have collaborated with scientists, programmers, and other personnel at Systems for Environmental Management (SEM), a private, non-profit research corporation, founded in Missoula, Montana, in 1977. Some of the earliest cooperative projects between the Fire Lab and SEM included climatology and fuel analysis studies.

Since that time, SEM staff have conducted further research for the Fire Lab on fuels and fire danger rating, participated in fire effects studies, designed databases, and written programs for many of the Fire Lab's computer applications. In fact, all of the Fire Lab systems accepted as operational, national, interagency fire management systems as of 2010 were developed in partnership with SEM:

- BehavePlus fire modeling system
- FlamMap fire mapping and analysis system
- FARSITE fire area simulator
- FOFEM first order fire effects model
- FireFamilyPlus historical analysis of fire danger and fire weather system
- WFAS, Wildland Fire Assessment System, web-based fire danger and fire weather system
- Citation Retrieval System, literature database for the Fire Effects Information System

New Tools for Fire Suppression

The thunder of giant airtankers taking off from western bases to drop retardant on hotspots or in front of advancing wildfires became a normal part of fire control efforts by the 1970s. Research by Fire Lab scientists in the suppression unit was an important part of making this form of aerial attack efficient and effective (Klade 2006).

While Fire Lab researchers pursued a better understanding of fire behavior, fire danger, and fuels, others initiated new and innovative research that used the Fire Lab's state-of-the-art facilities along with field studies to improve fire-retardant use and delivery. As Richard Rothermel recalled, the common retardant in the 1960s contained borate, which was found to be toxic to plants. Several new fire retardants had been introduced to the market, but little was known about which ones were the most effective. Rothermel, C.E. (Mike) Hardy, Charles (Chuck) George and others at the Fire Lab, including David Blakely, Cecelia (Ceci) Johnson, Greg Johnson and later Shirley Zilstra, working with researchers in California and Oregon, were assigned to use the Fire Lab's burn chamber to test retardants under controlled conditions of temperature, relative humidity, and fuel moisture. Retardants that showed promise were then tested in the wind tunnel, where wind speed was added to the other controlled variables. This research continues to guide many of the decisions made regarding aerial-applied retardants throughout the world.

In 1971, Jack Barrows presented a paper on retardant research at a symposium on the use of air operations to fight fire. According to Barrows, these experiments helped researchers better understand fire retardant effectiveness under various environmental and fuel conditions, and recommend different kinds of retardants for different fire conditions. Barrows noted that under "the more severe burning conditions with low humidity and moderate wind conditions long-term retardants are generally superior. The long-term retardants provide the greatest reduction in rate of fire spread after both one hour and three hours elapsed time following application" (Barrows 1971).

That same year, when Rothermel returned after a year at Colorado State University with a Master's degree in mechanical engineering, he wanted to return to researching fire behavior. But Rothermel had also trained as an aeronautical engineer, and interest had been growing nationally in applying military technologies to civilian applications. So upon his return, Barrows initially assigned Rothermel to work with Hardy and George on writing proposals to develop and test innovative tank-and-gating systems for fire retardant airplanes. Rothermel continued to interact with the researchers and the funders as needed, but once the project was underway, he returned to his work on fire behavior, while George continued testing fire retardants and delivery methods from the air.

As George later wrote, fire responders did not have access to good data on retardants or retardant application techniques, so instead they relied on "trial and error, experience and assessing what agencies preferred" (George and Fuchs 1991). With the goals of quantifying the application of retardants and improving drop efficiency and safety, George and his colleagues tested innovative "tank and gating system design, the properties of the fire retardant, and the relation between these two" with the goal of assuring "selection of the best aerial attack systems and to optimize their performance"(George 1975). George then translated these and other results into a simple slide calculator, reminiscent of Harry Gisborne's early fire danger rating meter, in which he integrated relationships between retardant volume, drop height, air speed, and aircraft type. Like other research at the Fire Lab, new knowledge about fire retardants was being packaged and delivered to managers as soon as possible after its development.

In 1966, Charles (Chuck) George worked on tests to screen and evaluate fire retardants (*photo: USDA Forest Service*).

Researchers used cups on the ground to test retardant coverage from aerial drops, starting in the mid-1960s (*photo: USDA Forest Service*).

Hand-held "computers" developed by Fire Lab researchers allowed pilots to quickly determine optimum coverage based on retardant volume, drop height, air speed, and aircraft type (*photo: USDA Forest Service*).

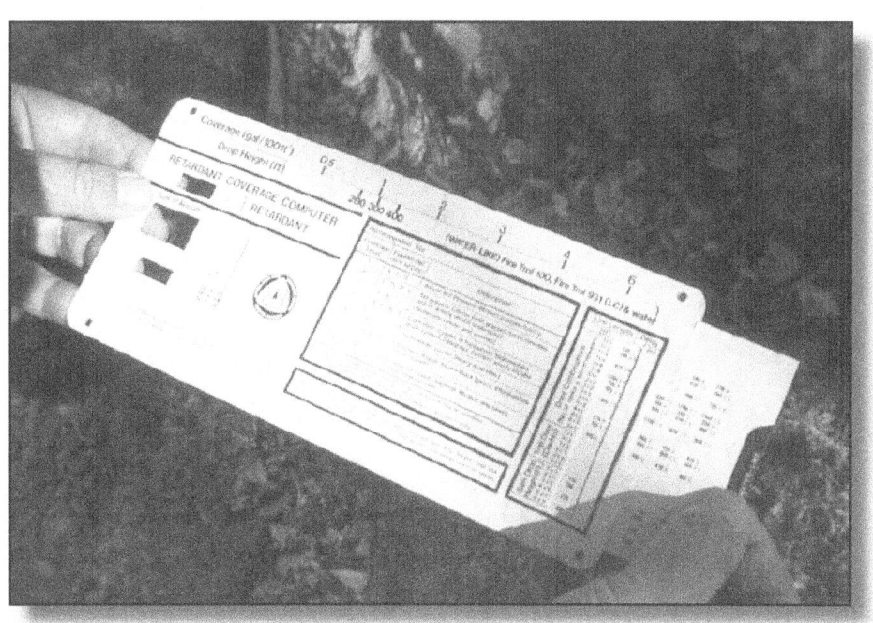

Scanning the Landscape for Fire

In 1964, [Stanley] Hirsch listed the attributes of an ideal fire monitoring remote sensing system: (1) detection of fire in its early stages; (2) effective operation day and night; and (3) ability to prioritize fires, distinguishing between dangerous fires and those of no significant consequence. Hirsch noted that the most important characteristic of a fire-mapping remote sensing system was the ability to detect fire size and location in relation to ground features (topography) and forest resources (vegetation and fuel).... Functionally, all the information must be communicated to fire management personnel for timely fire management decisions. Although these data timing issues were raised over 30 years ago, they are just beginning to be addressed by the fire suppression agencies (Ambrosia and others 1998).

In addition to developing successful fire retardants and methods to suppress fires, researchers also sought ways to locate fires as soon as possible after ignition. With the goal of extinguishing all fires by 10 a.m. the day after they were detected, fire managers needed better tools to identify

fires early. As Stanley (Stan) Hirsch explained, forest fires "spread slowly immediately after ignition" and during that period can be easily suppressed (Hirsch 1971). If fire managers could detect small fires even before they became visible to fire lookouts, then it would be easier, faster, and safer to respond to them, regardless of their location.

Thus, while one group of researchers measured and tested fuels in the new wind tunnel and controlled-burn chamber, others at the Fire Lab adapted and applied emerging technologies to reveal burning materials in the field: on the ground in remote locations, at night, and even in dense smoke, when traditional lookouts and other reporting systems might miss them (Cliff 1963). When electrical engineer Stan Hirsch first came to the Fire Lab from INEL in 1961, he began exploring his interests in infrared (IR) imagery within C.E. (Mike) Hardy's group. As Hardy recalled, it was clear that Hirsch's idea had great potential, so the Fire Lab soon spun it off into its own research program to investigate ways to locate and map fires when regular surveillance from lookout stations was impractical or impossible because of fire location, environmental conditions, or time of day. Hirsch worked with physicist Ralph Wilson, research forester Nonan Noste, and engineer Forrest Madden to apply this technology in research that became known as Project Fire Scan.

Stanley Hirsch (right) and pilot Stan Butryn of Project Fire Scan (*photo: USDA Forest Service*).

Physicist Ralph Wilson was instrumental in developing methods for using infrared systems to detect fires (*photo: USDA Forest Service*).

The idea, Hirsch later reported, was to use infrared scanners to detect fire "day or night and under conditions when smoke or other atmospheric pollutants prohibit visual detection." He also wanted to use infrared to "map the perimeter of large forest fires, determine the relative intensity along various portions of the fire front, detect spot fires outside of the main front, and determine the size and extent of unburned areas within the fire perimeter." With this information, fire managers could determine if a fire threatened a ranch or town, for example, or they could use the information to map escape routes for firefighters and people living near a fire. As Hirsch recalled, the goal was to be able to do these things from the air "without exposing personnel to the hazards of ground scouting in dangerous fire situations" (Hirsch 1971).

In the fall of 1962, Hirsch and his research team mapped a 300-acre controlled burn where a temperature inversion had trapped a layer of smoke 2,000 ft. deep in the valley. Despite these obstacles, according to the annual report from the Chief of the Forest Service, the infrared image could "see" through the smoke, indicating that the technology had potential for identifying and mapping fires. Further testing came in 1963, when researchers used infrared mapping on three wildfires to identify the perimeter, find hot spots, and locate spot fires outside the main fire perimeter, then relayed that information to the managers on the ground (Cliff 1964). Early research

programs in infrared surveillance had been conducted with military aircraft and pilots but, as Richard Klade noted in his history of the Intermountain Station, the resulting "Forest Service systems, the only ones in the world known to be designed and developed specifically for fire detection and mapping, were products of the creativity and hard work of Hirsch, Wilson, and other individuals" (Klade 2006).

Just as new technology was incorporated in the structure of the Fire Lab to answer questions about fire behavior, new technology was developed to answer the monitoring and mapping questions raised by Hirsch and his colleagues. At first, the researchers borrowed an infrared scanner, which they modified to meet the requirements of their study. Then in 1964, the Office of Civil Defense negotiated a contract to manufacture the first Fire Mapping Infrared Line Scanner for the Forest Service, which they delivered in 1965 (http:// www.nifc.gov/NIICD/infrared/infrared.html).

During the fire seasons of 1963, 1964, and 1966, researchers worked at night and/or under heavy smoke cover to test the infrared system's ability to detect and map 38 forest fires and obtain information on the fire perimeter, the relative intensity of the fire, and spot fire locations. Fires ranging in size from 10 to over 200,000 acres were mapped by the scanner and photographed using Polaroid cameras. The photos taken from the scanner were either dropped directly into a fire camp that night from the aircraft or delivered to the fire camp from a landing area by vehicle. Thus, long before satellites provided instant communications in remote locations, Fire Lab scientists were using the best technology available to deliver information to managers within minutes to hours of an infrared flight. With this information, fire managers could identify the most critical areas of the fire, plan for safety zones or evacuations, locate spot fires needing attention, and prioritize areas for control the next morning (Cliff 1968). With the potential to scan 3,000 square miles per hour from the air compared with 600 square miles using traditional visual surveillance, the Fire Scan program was transferred into the Forest Service's fire protection program in 1966, even though testing continued.

While developing the capability to map fires using infrared technology, Project Fire Scan researchers also worked on identifying fires so small that they might be missed initially by lookouts and other on-the-ground detection systems. To address this problem, Ralph Wilson, Nonan Noste, and Forrest Madden combined the sophisticated technology of aerial detection with a very simple technology. They made artificial "fire targets" that closely mimicked the heat released from a small fire, using 14-inch buckets filled with sand and topped with burning charcoal. Planes equipped with infrared viewers patrolled areas near Missoula and other mountainous areas with different forest types looking for—and finding— the targets (Wilson and Noste 1966).

Using a bucket and charcoal, research forester Nonan Noste prepares a spot fire for testing aerial infrared detection systems in 1962 (*photo: USDA Forest Service*).

A 2-month follow-up test of an 8,000 square mile area adjacent to Missoula demonstrated that researchers had refined their ability to detect fires using infrared technology. In the summer of 1970, the Fire Scan program successfully mapped more than 200 wildfires, 45 of which were detected before they were reported by lookouts and other patrol aircraft. However, the technology had limitations. While the IR systems picked up some fires so small they were actually campfires, in other instances they missed wildfires detected visually. As Hirsch noted, "[u]ntil we learn more about the relationship between heat output and smoke output from latent fires we cannot determine the relative effectiveness of visual and IR systems" (Hirsch 1971).

Hirsch expressed confidence that "IR used in combination with visual detection will result in a more efficient system than visual [detection] alone." According to Richard Rothermel, field personnel never fully implemented Fire Scan's fire detection capabilities, in part because of the limitations of real-time communication (Rothermel, personal communication 2010). Nevertheless, the fire mapping capabilities proved to be highly successful and two IR-equipped planes are still dispatched from Boise, Idaho, as part of the National Interagency Fire Center's National Infrared Operation (NIROPS) unit.

The Ecology of Fire and Wildlands

The Wilderness Act of 1964 called for managing wilderness areas for their natural qualities ... but one of the most unnatural acts we'd been committing in the wild all these years was suppression of fire (Mutch 2009).

Gifford Pinchot and many of his contemporaries understood the beneficial role fire has played in maintaining the health of the nation's forests. These ecological benefits include the creation of wildlife habitat, increased availability of soil nutrients, improved growth of old-growth trees, and the regeneration of forests. In addition, naturally occurring fire can improve long-term watershed and environmental conditions, create more resilient ecosystems, and even protect forests from more intense fires in the future (Cones and Keller 2008).

Widespread settlement of forested areas in the late 19th and early 20th centuries, coupled with the post-1910 commitment to firefighting upon which Forest Service policy was based, left many forests, particularly in the Rocky Mountain West and the Southeast, without regular fires. Ironically, this left some forests more at risk for severe fires and possibly more vulnerable to disease and insect infestations than they would have been with more frequent fires. With more and more people choosing to live and work in or near the edges of public wildlands, managers were under increased pressure to find ways to better protect the health of a forest without putting lives at risk or threatening property or national landmarks.

This situation challenged fire managers to find a balance between human safety and infrastructure protection and the overall health of the forests. Fire Lab scientist Robert (Bob) Mutch and David Aldrich, a forester for the Bitterroot National Forest, began to investigate how to allow fire to play its natural role in the nation's wildlands, particularly those newly designated as wilderness by the Wilderness Act of 1964. As part of a study initiated in 1970, the two men tested a new approach to fire management in a 100-square-mile area in the White Cap Creek drainage in

Fire management pioneers in 2002, 30 years after the White Cap study was approved: Bob Mutch (left) with Bill Worf, Bud Moore, Orville Daniels, Dave Aldrich, and Doris Milner (President of the Montana Wilderness Association when the White Cap plan was approved). Forest Service regional directors Worf and Moore initiated the White Cap research project and enlisted the support of Daniels, who was then the Supervisor of the Bitterroot National Forest. They then assigned Mutch and Aldrich to conduct the study (*photo: Robert Mutch*).

Idaho chosen for its remoteness, diverse topography, and varied forest types. As Mutch recalled, they spent a year "sampling vegetation, collecting evidence of fire history, studying records of past fires, and charting the effects of fire exclusion" (Wells 2009).

Aldrich and Mutch divided the test area into ecological zones, with different fire prescriptions and management options written for each zone. While this new approach to fire management needed to provide fire managers with guidelines on how to handle different types of fires within the test area, they also had to ensure public safety and prevent major adverse effects outside the management area (Klade 2006). In the summer of 1972, their plan for the White Cap area was ready and, after a briefing in Washington, DC, Forest Service Chief John McGuire approved it.

Three weeks after the plan was signed, the new approach, which Mutch described as "this radical idea of letting nature do its thing," was put to the test. In the summer of 1972, a small fire was spotted in Bad Luck Creek within the study area and was allowed to burn. That fire put itself out after 4 days, burning less than one quarter of an acre. The following year, a fire in the Fritz Creek drainage burned about 1,600 acres, "more than had been burned by all the previous fires of record in the [White Cap] drainage" (Wells 2009). When the fire moved beyond the test area, fire fighters suppressed it. Even though the fire attracted some negative media attention, intimating that "the shift from fire management meant Smokey Bear was laying down his shovel," researchers documented positive effects of the fire on vegetation and wildlife, and the first major test of the new policy was deemed a success (McGuire 1975).

Based in part on innovative programs such as the one conducted by Mutch and Aldrich, Assistant Secretary of Agriculture M. Rupert Cutler announced a major shift in Forest Service policy in 1978. In the future, he said, "some forest fires which start on National Forest System lands will be used for predetermined beneficial purposes rather than being put out immediately" (Carle 2002). Although application of this new policy in the field proved challenging, this announcement ended both the 10 a.m. rule and, in effect, the legacy of the 1910 fires.

Reevaluating the History of Fire

Concepts of forestry were developed in moist regions of Europe for the purpose of reestablishing trees on land deforested centuries earlier. Early European foresters considered fire entirely a destructive force introduced by humans. We now know that most North American forests as well as ancient forests in Europe were shaped over thousands of years by distinctive patterns of fire (Arno 2005).

With a new policy in place to allow fire to resume its natural role in shaping some of the nation's forests, managers needed guidelines to make informed decisions about where fire should be allowed to burn and under what conditions. To contribute to this understanding and help provide these guidelines, ecologist Stephen (Steve) Arno initiated a study to better understand the frequency, intensity, and influence of fire on different forest types in the Rocky Mountain West. In a study of forested areas of the Bitterroot National Forest, for example, Arno and others looked for evidence of past fires by documenting fire scars on living trees, and then analyzing the role fire played in forest development before fires in the West began to be aggressively suppressed (Klade 2006). Arno gradually expanded this study into locations outside the Bitterroot, concluding that lightning-caused and human-started fires were a major agent of change throughout the northern Rocky Mountain forests.

As he dug deeper into the fire histories of forests throughout the West, it became clear to Arno that these wildlands needed fire to survive. "Forests are processes, not just trees and plants," Arno noted. "And these forests can't survive and remain healthy without processes such as fire." Comparing nature to the workings of a clock, he compared removing fire from a forest to removing a gear from the clock. "Of course, you can't remove the gear and expect the clock to work, yet people expect nature to work without fire," he said (Stilling 2005).

As Arno's work documented, when fires are routinely suppressed in forests that historically saw frequent fire, they become dense with shade-tolerant species and wildlife lose critical habitat. Keeping fire out of wildlands can also result in health-related problems for trees and other plants, such as insect infestations and disease epidemics, as well as increased potential for severe fires in these forests.

As the evidence continued to grow about the critical role fire plays in forest ecology, the Forest Service continued to reconsider its policy regarding fire. Perhaps most telling, by the late 1970s the Division of Fire Control had become the new Division of Fire Management. Although on the surface this may seem to be simply a bureaucratic move, Richard Klade points out that the "implications of this name change were huge," suggesting for the first time that fire should not just be controlled, but it should also be managed for the well-being of the forests themselves (Klade 2006). And then came the fire season of 1988, and everything researchers thought they knew about fires and fire behavior was put to the test.

Letting Fires Burn

Understanding fire ecology principles is absolutely essential in developing appropriate fire management strategies for fire-dependent ecosystems in wilderness. Knowledge of the continental pattern of fire regimes will equip us to plan wilderness fire management

Bob Mutch and Dave Aldrich (left to right) hiking the White Cap drainage in 1970 (*photo: Bud Moore, BLM*)

programs that take into account fire history, fire regime elements, and fire effects (Mutch 1995).

With the passage of the Wilderness Act in 1964, the National Park Service and the Forest Service began to look for ways to allow areas designated as wilderness to continue "untrammeled by man" and without interference or "active" management. To this end, in the late 1960s, the Northern Region designated a remote area of the Bitterroot National Forest as a test site for allowing fire to burn naturally within its borders under specific conditions. Fire Lab researcher Robert (Bob) Mutch and forester Dave Aldrich, who worked for the national forests, were chosen to lead the project.

The two men spent a year documenting the diverse vegetation types and the history of fire in the test area. Drawing on research at the Fire Lab to help determine likely rates of spread in the test area, they presented a plan in 1972 to the Chief of the Forest Service, who approved it without reservation. While a fire did escape the test area that following summer, Mutch recalled that because they had a concise plan in place and they followed it, Forest Service management was satisfied with the results. Indeed, several other national forests followed their lead and established policies to allow fire to resume its natural place throughout the nation's wildlands.

In 2006, Mutch received the Harold Biswell Lifetime Achievement Award from the Association for Fire Ecology, in part for his 1970 article in *Ecology* that argues that "fire-dependent plant communities burn more readily than non-fire-dependent communities because natural selection has favored development of characteristics that make them more flammable" and for his leadership in developing the 1972 White Cap Fire Management Plan in the Selway-Bitterroot Wilderness.

Thinking Ecologically

Once we started looking at ecologically based management, with habitat types and other tools for looking at the ecology of forests in the 1970s, then more and more field foresters and foresters at all levels were saying we should not just be managing these forests as if they were plantations and tree farms (Arno 2010).

After completing a PhD in forest ecology from the University of Montana in the early 1970s, Stephen (Steve) Arno first worked on a ranger district for a few months and then for the Forestry Sciences Lab in Missoula, inventorying habitat types of Montana forests. As part of that assignment, he tracked the fire history of each stand. As he recalled, more than 70 percent of all the forests he and his colleagues sampled—from ponderosa pine to cedar and hemlock—showed evidence of previous fires, and yet these stands also showed signs of trees having survived the fires.

Because of his interest, Arno was assigned to work part time with Bob Mutch, Bill Fischer, and others on the effects of fire, before eventually transferring to the Fire Lab fulltime. The more research he conducted in the field, the more Arno came to appreciate the positive and complex

Steve Arno (right) and forester Clint Carlson explain how a ponderosa pine fire scar reveals a 300-year history of frequent surface fires that helped maintain open park-like ponderosa pine forests with a grassy understory (*photo: USDA Forest Service*).

role fire played in the ecosystems of the northern Rocky Mountains. For example, fires would kill the more fire-susceptible species with thin bark and few adaptations to fire, whereas fire-resistant trees like ponderosa pines would survive. Indeed, these species actually need fire to maintain a presence—as do the wildlife that rely on the habitat that fires help maintain. Thus, it became clear that by removing fire, land managers were in fact harming the very lands they were attempting to protect.

In 2004, Arno received the Harold Biswell Lifetime Achievement Award from the Association for Fire Ecology in part for his pioneering research on fire history that resulted in major advances in knowledge of the role of fire in the northern Rocky Mountains and his work advocating for restoration of fire-adapted ecosystems.

Recalling the Yellowstone Fires of 1988

June 14, 1988: A small fire starts on Storm Creek, just north of Yellowstone National Park. . . . The Storm Creek Fire and many other fires would keep burning in Yellowstone until cool, wet weather arrived in the fall. Now legendary, the 'Summer of Fire' brought people, science, and wild nature together like never before or since (National Park Service 2008).

In 1988, fires in Yellowstone National Park burned close to a million acres and put at risk some of the nation's most beloved cultural treasures. While Yellowstone did not lose any of its historic buildings to fire, the high winds and low humidity led to a much more severe and faster-moving fire than experts predicted, pushing fire policy, fire spread models, and even public relations to or beyond their capacity. No model existed for predicting the behavior of wind-driven crown fires.

In July of that year, when Yellowstone managers had already made the decision not to suppress some lightning-caused fires in the Park, Richard Rothermel, Bob Burgan, Roberta Bartlette and others from the Fire Lab in Missoula traveled to Yellowstone as part of a team to predict a worst-case scenario for the spread of fire. But as soon as the researchers had predictions in hand, the fire exceeded them. As Rothermel later explained, "we couldn't come up with a worst-case scenario because ... the winds came again and again and again, and the worst case happened almost weekly.... It was an amazing season," he recalled. "Nobody had seen this combination of weather and fires before" (Wells 2008).

Like the fires of 1910, the hot, wind-driven fires that raged through the Yellowstone ecosystem in 1988 captured the nation's attention. Stories about the fire ran on the front pages of newspapers and were covered on network news, initiating an often passionate debate about the role fire plays in the health and wellbeing of the nation's wildlands. The Yellowstone fires climaxed with a "blow up" on August 20, 1988—incidentally, the same day of the Big Blow Up of 1910—displaying fire behavior unexpected even by seasoned fire managers and scientists. The fires were carried by strong winds from stand to stand, spotted profusely, and could not be stopped by roads, waterways, or miles of fireline.

While these extreme conditions are indeed rare, or "worst case," Rothermel realized that he needed to "expand his model so that managers on the ground could better predict the risks associated with these kinds of extreme fire conditions...." Determined to produce such a predictive tool before he retired, Rothermel turned his attention back to research (Klade 2006).

To effectively predict and prepare for crown fires, two questions needed to be answered, according to Rothermel:

- Under what conditions is a crown fire likely to occur?
- What is the expected size and intensity of an anticipated crown fire?

Forest Service and other researchers outside the Fire Lab recently had addressed the first question, so Rothermel set to work on the second (Rothermel 1991).

In this case, however, the Fire Lab's research facilities were of limited use, since Rothermel could not reproduce crown-fire conditions in the burn chamber or wind tunnels. So like Gifford Pinchot, Harry Gisborne, and Jack Barrows before him, Rothermel turned instead to the historical record, gathering and analyzing data from the records of extreme fires in the region. He also had access to a wealth of existing studies by Fire Lab researchers. For example, Jim Brown and other researchers at the Fire Lab had been investigating ways to describe the fuels and fire behavior potential of tree crowns. And just the year before, in 1987, Rothermel himself had completed a study of why, during especially dry years, tree crowns are at particular risk of burning. He drew on all of these data as the basis for modeling crown fire behavior.

In 1991, Rothermel published a new model for predicting the behavior and size of crown fires in the Northern Rocky Mountains, producing it as a workbook that decision makers could use in the field to "rapidly assess probable behavior from on-site observations without the aid of a computer." Building on Frank Albini's work and his own experiences in the classroom, Rothermel introduced the model using nomograms. These graphical representations for decision makers were based on five moisture conditions in the field: early spring before greenup, late spring or early summer after greenup, a normal dry summer, summer drought, and late summer severe drought (Rothermel

The Yellowstone Fires of 1988 led to new research questions about how to predict crown fires, particularly under extreme weather conditions. (*photos: Jeff Henry, National Park Service*).

1991). Rothermel's model, along with theories of crown fires developed in Canada, still forms the basis for many crown fire behavior systems in use today (Alexander and others 2006). Having met this final professional goal, Rothermel retired from the Fire Lab in 1994, 33 years after he first came to Missoula from Idaho Falls.

Big Picture: Fire and Fire Effects

The Fire Effects Information System works on synthesizing research nationwide. Many of our scientists and professionals also produce excellent synthesis work. In addition, the Fire Lab is committed to regional and national training, in both the classroom and developing national curricula. We believe our investment in training and outreach is higher than anywhere else in the country (C. C. Hardy 2010).

As fire science and forest and fire management policy evolved, forest managers needed access to information that summarized the best of this knowledge in forms that are accessible and usable in the field. Richard Rothermel, Frank Albini, Patricia Andrews, Bob Burgan, Mark Finney, and others at the Fire Lab focused on distilling new fire behavior knowledge into numeric and graphical representations. They produced handbooks and eventually computer programs and technologies to transfer the latest understanding of fire science into user-friendly and field-applicable guides.

Researchers working on the effects of fire have taken a different approach. In 1977, for example, Stephen Arno, as part of a small team led by Robert Pfister, collaborated with national forest scientists in Montana to produce a handbook of forest habitat types in the state. Forester Bill Fischer initiated several publications describing fire ecology based on habitat types of various parts of the northern Rockies and Great Basin. These researchers understood that forest managers need consistent descriptions of plant communities and their relationships with fire if they are to communicate across disciplines and make informed management decisions, including how and when to use prescribed fire or allow naturally occurring fires.

In 1985, before widespread availability of the Internet, Fire Lab researchers Jim Brown, Bill Fischer, and Pete Taylor conceived of a Fire Effects Information System to

Reviewing the Literature

Fire Effects Information System is Born

The real challenge is getting the information to managers in an easy fashion so they aren't overwhelmed. A lot of our fire effects information work was done trying to make all this technical knowledge available to managers in a way that is relevant to their job and easy to obtain. This involved a combination of summarizing the knowledge like the Fire Effects Information System and developing models (Brown 2010).

Jim Brown joined the Fire Lab in 1965 as he was completing a doctorate in forestry. As an expert on the quantification of fuels, Brown focused on developing fuel models and other methods for predicting and inventorying fuels. For the White Cap test area and eventually other national forests preparing fire management plans, he trained crews to inventory fuels so they could determine fire potential. He also developed a method to estimate tree crown fuel, which was used as part of Richard Rothermel's model for crown fire behavior.

After working in fuels for the first half of his career, in the 1980s Brown joined the Fire Lab's fire effects research team, investigating the effect of fire on aspen stands. As he worked with Stephen Arno, Bill Fischer and others on the effects of fire, Brown and his colleagues realized that a wealth of new knowledge about fire effects was available to land managers. The problem was that they needed to sort through stacks of studies before they could use the knowledge to make informed decisions. With this in mind, the Fire Lab established a Fire Effects Information System to review, evaluate, and then synthesize the best of the literature so that managers didn't have to locate the information and analyze it on their own. This program continues to this day, covering more than 1,000 species and including a library of more than 60,000 documents.

In 1993, Chief Dale Roberson presented Jim Brown with the Forest Service's Superior Science Award for "numerous contributions to wildland fire management and modern forest policy."

Jim Brown gathering fuel samples in the spring of 1972. Brown has been referred to as "the foremost wildland fuels person in the United States, and probably the world" (*photo: USDA Forest Service*).

provide literature reviews through an interactive computer program operating on the Forest Service's computer network for use by in-house managers and practitioners. They initially proposed covering the basic biology and fire ecology of species in the Great Basin, but after the fire season of 1988, their vision expanded to include species throughout the continental United States. By 1995, when the expanded database became available "online" and easily accessible by the public as well as managers, it contained literature reviews covering more than 1,000 species. In addition to concise overviews of the literature, this work also resulted in a national resource of approximately 60,000 carefully key-worded articles. Ecologist and FEIS manager Jane Kapler Smith believes the Fire Lab FEIS library is the best literature collection on basic ecology relating to fire and fire effects in the world (Smith, personal communication 2010).

The FEIS ecologists and writers have synthesized the literature on nearly 1,200 species. However, their work is not over. With growing concerns about invasive species as well as global climate change, new research continues to be added to the wealth of knowledge that practitioners in the field need. The FEIS synthesizers continue to review new research as it becomes available and revisit older species reviews to ensure they provide state-of-the-art information to managers.

Analyzing the Effects of Fire

We will not have adequate fire management until all activities of a fire organization—including prevention, control, and beneficial uses of fire—are directed by land management objectives. Because it cuts across so many resource management boundaries and affects both short-term and long-term resource outputs, the only effective way to deal with fire is on a multi-resource, multi-objective basis. Further, because fire does not respect property boundaries, planning must consider the objectives of all landowners involved (Lotan 1979).

Conducting fire research in the field poses a constant challenge to researchers, with so many variables—from weather to fuels—difficult to measure and control. In 1966, Fire Lab

Communicating to Professionals and the Public

Fire is such a charismatic issue, that it's possible to draw people in and teach them about science. We've reached out to two or three thousand children over the last ten years, teaching them that science is a process of creative and critical thinking. If we've enhanced their understanding of science even a little bit then it has all been worthwhile (Smith 2010).

In the mid-1970s, Jane Kapler (later Kapler Smith) entered the Fire Lab for the first time to meet with Bob Mutch. As a temporary employee of the National Park Service, she had written an environmental assessment of the historical role of fire in Glacier National Park and related ecosystems, and now she was looking for advice. As she walked down the hall looking for Bob Mutch's office, she read the names on the office doors: Andrews, Arno, Brown, Burgan, Rothermel, and Mutch. "They were the names straight from my bibliography," she recalled.

After several more visits to the Fire Lab to meet with researchers and attend seminars, she knew her career path was set. But she also knew she would need a graduate degree in forest ecology to follow it, so she left Montana to attend Colorado State University to research the effects of fire on aspen groves.

When she returned to Missoula in 1991, Kapler Smith soon found herself back at the Fire Lab, writing reports—first on the fire ecology of the habitats of Northern Idaho as a contractor and then, in 1994, working for the Fire Effects Information System (FEIS). As she recalls, she inherited a vision that was ahead of its time. Now as the leader of FEIS, she and her colleagues continue to build on that vision as more and more land managers need access to quality information to make informed decisions based on the ecological effects of fire.

Jane Kapler Smith (kneeling right) explains the effects of fire to three generations of visitors during an open house at the Fire Lab in 2004. Although the Fire Lab was established to conduct research, education and training for both professionals and the general public have been an integral part of Lab activities almost from the very beginning (*photo: USDA Forest Service*).

researchers William Beaufait, C.E. (Mike) Hardy, William Fischer, and others set out to test the effects of burning and silvicultural treatments on forests dominated by spruce, fir, and larch. This effort became known as the Miller Creek-Newman Ridge project. The scientists measured how fire affected air quality, vegetation development, conifer regeneration, water quality, erosion, and small animal populations (Latham and others 1998). This research was one of the first fire studies to replicate field experiments over a variety of environmental conditions, using a rigorous approach to field research on fire effects. The research helped initiate establishment of the Miller Creek Demonstration Forest on the Flathead National Forest, which serves as a "living laboratory" for forestry research to this day. A second extensive field study began at the Lubrecht Experimental Forest in 1972, where fire was combined with silvicultural practices for management of forests dominated by ponderosa pine and Douglas-fir.

The Miller Creek-Newman Ridge and Lubrecht studies demonstrated the feasibility and importance of field research into fire ecology. Based on these successes, the Fire Lab launched an extensive Research, Development and Applications (RD&A) Program in 1974 to focus specifically on fire's ecological effects. This move marked a major shift in Fire Lab research, which had, up to that point, focused on understanding, predicting, and ultimately controlling fire. The new RD&A program, on the other hand, took an interdisciplinary approach to determining the effects of fire on ecosystems and applying this knowledge to management. As Jim Lotan, who headed the new program, explained in an article in *Environmental Management* (1979), the Fire Effects RD&A included laboratory work, field studies, and software development to improve the land manager's capability to integrate fire management considerations into land-use planning.

The RD&A program in turn led to new fire effects models, including FOFEM (First Order Fire Effects Model), developed by Elizabeth Reinhardt, Robert Keane, and others, for predicting tree mortality, fuel consumption, smoke production, and soil heating, as well as the Fire Effects Information System. FOFEM was designed to help natural resource managers make better-informed decisions when planning how to best protect the nation's wildlands. Another model, FireBGCv2, has been developed by Robert Keane to simulate the interactions of weather and climate, vegetation growth, disturbances such as fire and insect infestations, and management activities across landscapes.

The 1970s also marked the beginning of Fire Lab research into fire history, including Stephen Arno's studies (discussed above) and now, more recent studies by Emily Heyerdahl and colleagues to investigate spatial and temporal variation in fire history using the science of dendrochronology (or tree rings). The use of dendrochronology has provided a window into the deep past of many forests, enabling researchers to better understand the long-term role that climate and other factors have played in fire occurrence, fire behavior, and vegetation patterns. The results have immediate relevance for natural resource managers as they plan for potential effects of climate change.

Thinking Globally about the Long-Term Effects of Fire

In 2001, [Wei Min] Hao decided to develop a nationwide system to monitor in near real-time the distribution of active fires throughout space (across the land) and time, fire severity, burned areas, and smoke dispersions using the latest satellite remote sensing technology…. The information is critical … in formulating daily firefighting strategies, resource allocation, and predicting air quality (Anjozian 2009).

While most of the Fire Lab's work has focused on research questions regarding wildland fires in the United States, some research has been, of necessity, international in scope. Large-scale fires in South America or Africa, for example, can directly affect air quality and climate around the world, and contribute to the accumulation of atmospheric pollutants and greenhouse gases in the atmosphere, which is a growing global concern.

In 1987, the Fire Lab established a new research unit to begin investigating the chemistry of fire, including the production of smoke resulting from wildfires. While smoke associated with wildland fires can pose serious pollution and health-related problems in the continental United States, fires started deliberately by farmers, loggers, large commercial interests and others to clear land in Central and South America, Africa, and Southeast Asia contribute approximately 80 percent of all fire-related pollution each year. To better understand the extent of fire-related pollution and its long-term effects on air quality and greenhouse gasses, therefore, researchers need to look at fires around the globe.

In 1991, Fire Lab chemists Darold Ward and Wei Min Hao began working in partnership with NASA on designing and implementing field studies to measure the effects of human-caused fires. Starting in Brazil and South Africa, the researchers set up numerous decade-long field experiments to collect and analyze the composition of smoke produced by these fires. Like their other colleagues at the Fire Lab, the researchers did not design the experiments to directly affect public policy, but rather to provide scientific data to other scientists and the international policy community so that they could make more informed decisions about the impacts of fires on regional and global air quality and climate.

Since that time, Hao and his research team have expanded these studies into similar investigations of fires in Mexico,

Russia, Canada, and the continental United States, using remote sensing data from satellites—in essence expanding their research from sampling instruments on the ground into studies that stretch over time and space. They also are investigating the long-term air-quality effects of fires in Siberia where global climate change could have a major impact, as seen in the Russian wildfires of 2010.

Hao's work on questions like these led to his involvement, starting in 1994, with the United Nation's Intergovernmental Panel for Climate Change, which enlisted scientists from around the world to better understand the long-term effects of climate change. Hao's contributions focused on developing a methodology to quantify nitrous oxide, methane, and other greenhouse gases produced by fires in different ecosystems. As a member of the Intergovernmental Panel on Climate Change, Hao and his fellow panel members were awarded the Nobel Peace Prize in 2007 for their "efforts to build up and disseminate greater knowledge about man-made climate change, and to lay the foundations for the measures that are needed to counteract such change" (Nobel Prize 2007).

Looking to the Future

Our research facilities are uncharacteristically well maintained and are still highly relevant today, partly due to the pride that every incumbent in this building has had in this place. And it's partly due to the incredible foresight and the engineering that went into building it. Our combustion chamber and two wind tunnels were state of the science in 1960 and are still very nearly state of the science today (C.C. Hardy 2010).

Trained as an engineer, Richard Rothermel approached fire research as he would any engineering problem, with the assumption that the researcher will come up with an answer. That was a given from the very beginning. So the researcher does whatever is necessary to get that answer. For example, when attempting to understand fire behavior, Rothermel and his colleagues applied what was known about the physics of the problem, and then conducted experiments to fill in where the underlying physics was not known. When this process revealed gaps, the researchers made assumptions, put the model together, and then tested it to see how well it performed. This was an iterative process, but the goal was ultimately to produce an answer and deliver results of the project to wildland managers.

Such an approach suggests that fire research has, by its very nature, a beginning, a middle, and eventually an end. But fire research has a way of taking on a life of its own, when what one knew in the past simply is not adequate to respond to current events or conditions. After the fires of 1910, the

Continuing a Family Tradition

Fire danger is weather driven, and Dad's early work on fire weather was for fire danger rating. One of my early projects at the Fire Lab was working with Bob Burgan on using satellite data to 'measure' the condition of vegetation moisture using visible wave-lengths of light. Those reflected wavelengths to the satellite allowed us to calculate indexes that related to the condition of the vegetation and contributed to our ability to map fire danger nationally (C.C. Hardy 2010).

Fire danger rating depends on precise weather data. When C.E. (Mike) Hardy was assigned to work on the rating system in the early 1950s, he looked for ways to improve data gathering, often bringing home weather instrumentation to work on after hours. As he worked, his son Colin Hardy often "shadowed him," trying to assist as his father tried out different kinds of stands and instrumentation. Colin vividly recalls working in the lab as early as 1961, washing beakers and helping out after hours.

As Mike Hardy no doubt hoped at the time, these and other experiences made a strong and lasting impression on his son. Years later, Colin graduated with an interdisciplinary degree in resource conservation, and eventually completed a doctorate in forestry, with an emphasis on remote sensing of wildland fires. Thus Colin Hardy, now the Program Manager for all the research conducted at the Fire Lab, continued a family tradition of research and adapting new technologies to better understand wildland fires.

Colin and Mike Hardy, two generations of wildland fire researchers, c. 1954 (*photo: Colin Hardy*).

fledgling Forest Service realized how even one fire can shape public opinion. In much the same way, environmental concerns like global climate change and large-scale fires like those in Yellowstone have led to new research questions and demands for new management tools.

In addition, as more sophisticated instrumentation and measurement tools become available, researchers of today and tomorrow can pursue questions that were impossible to study, perhaps even impossible to articulate, in 1960. As Colin Hardy explained, in some ways it is as if the Fire Lab has backed up and started over, applying new capabilities to investigate a new theory and then testing the theory in the laboratory or in the field. For example, existing fire behavior models assume that energy moves from one particle to the next through radiant heat transfer, but researchers are now conducting very basic research, investigating the role of convection in igniting that second particle, as well as examining the role turbulence plays in heat transfer (C. C. Hardy, personal communication 2010).

Climate change adds to the host of questions the next generation of fire researchers needs to address. As ecosystems appear to be shifting in response to changed climate patterns, the fate of North American forests and other wildlands is uncertain. Managers now use fire to improve the health and sustainability of many wildland ecosystems with fire-dependent species. But if the climate changes, fundamental knowledge of the relationship between fire, species and ecosystem resilience may not apply in the same way. Managers will need new knowledge to better understand the complex interactions of fire and ecosystems, and insights into how existing knowledge can be applied in different ways.

In the meantime, grasses, shrubs, and trees continue to grow in many ecosystems that historically were shaped by frequent fire. According to Stephen Arno, duff, litter, and downed woody material continue to accumulate, and many formerly open forests have grown into dense expanses of continuous forest with shrubs and small trees providing "ladders" of fuel from ground to treetop. This can become a highly flammable environment under the right conditions. "If warming trends continue," Arno noted, "and there's no reason to think that they won't, the handwriting is clearly on the wall...."(Arno, personal communication 2010).

Like the fires of 1910 and 1988 and the launching of Sputnik in 1957, external events such as global climate change may catalyze future innovations in fire science. If weather patterns change, creating longer and drier summers in some areas, then the fire season will probably become longer and potentially more dangerous. And yet, if managers exclude fires altogether from wildlands where they used to occur frequently, the forests may be doubly stressed by changing climate and by increasingly dense vegetation and fuels. Thus, managers continue to look to research to help them maintain healthy ecosystems and to help them better understand fire and forest ecology. For example, managers and researchers alike may ask new questions of the National Fire Danger Rating System, particularly if the fire season starts earlier in the spring and lasts longer in the fall.

As in the past, new technology—especially computing power and communication capabilities—will allow researchers and managers to explore innovative ideas in fire management and hypothetical outcomes. Much as Frank Albini's nomograms provided practitioners with a visual tool for predicting fire behavior, computer visualization tools allow researchers to present data in ways that are easier to understand and interpret. These capabilities can be integrated into existing models and systems like BehavePlus and FARSITE, or they can be developed into tools that managers can use to make more informed decisions by graphically illustrating alternative decisions. Satellite imagery also provides new data for assessing air quality and fire danger, while providing better visualization tools for decision makers.

Models and systems also grow or change as new knowledge becomes available. As more and more sophisticated models and systems have been developed, however, some don't fit together very well, according to Patricia Andrews. As the Fire Lab celebrated its 50th anniversary in 2010, Andrews and others are looking for ways to go back to the basic mathematical model building blocks to create modular programs that will make it easier to incorporate new research as it becomes available, while also more effectively integrating fire behavior, fire effects, weather, and smoke modeling systems. "We're not going to run out of work anytime soon," she said (Andrews, personal communication 2010).

People Stop and Pay Attention
When He Tells Them to Beware

The fundamental work initiated in the early 1960s at the Northern Forest Fire Research Laboratory has reaped many rewards, from sophisticated models for predicting fire behavior, to tools for understanding the critical role fire plays in ensuring the resilience and sustainability of the nation's wildlands. But perhaps the most visible legacy of the Fire Lab's research over the past 50 years is the Smokey Bear sign that greets visitors to state and national forests, alerting them to the fire danger for that day.

That rating, ranging from "low" to "extreme," is still basically determined by the fuel, topography, and weather, or what Harry Gisborne first called the fire environment triangle. The signage suggests that the rating is based on Smokey's intuition or friendly guess, but it is actually based largely on research produced by the Fire Lab. Each day, the danger rating is calculated using data from the network of weather stations first proposed by Gisborne and originally equipped with portable weather equipment constructed by C.E. (Mike) Hardy and his associates. Calculations come from the models and systems developed by John Deeming, Jack Cohen, Larry Bradshaw, and their colleagues, incorporating the fuel models developed by Jim Brown, Hal Anderson, and others, and the greenness indexes adapted by Bob Burgan, Bobbie Bartlette, and their colleagues at the Fire Lab. Without this sound basis in science, Smokey Bear would not have the information needed to predict that day's danger.

As Jack Barrows noted, "had it not been for ... the pioneering work done at the [F]ire [L]ab at Missoula by Rothermel and others to develop a mathematical model of fire behavior, we wouldn't see the fire danger rating system as it is now. So these things have a tendency to develop periodically and they can be applied to other lines of research and that's exactly what happened in fire danger rating" (Barrows 1976).

Indeed, the pioneering research conducted at the Fire Sciences Laboratory in Missoula laid the groundwork for much of what is known today about the fundamentals of fire behavior and fire effects, resulting in increased forest protection, firefighter safety, and overall forest health. To ensure that the public protects its national forests and is informed about the risk of starting an accidental fire, the national fire danger map, based on Fire Lab research, continues to contribute to the fire danger rating sign Smoky Bear monitors to this day.

The Smokey Bear Fire Danger Rating Sign greets visitors to most state and national forests (*photo: USDA Forest Service*).

Fire Lab History: Timeline of Key Events

1891—Congress gives the President the power to set aside public lands "with timber or undergrowth, whether of commercial value or not, as public reservations…."

1898—Department of Agriculture appoints Gifford Pinchot, known as the first American-born forester, to head the Division of Forestry. During his first year, Pinchot establishes a Section of Special Investigations, a research arm, and initiates a major study of wildfires in the United States.

1905—President Theodore Roosevelt signs the Transfer Act, establishing the Forest Service within the U.S. Department of Agriculture, with Gifford Pinchot the agency's Chief Forester.

1910—Fires burn more than 3 million acres in Washington, Idaho, and Montana. The Forest Service, now under the leadership of Pinchot protégé Henry Graves, strengthens its policy to suppress fires.

1915—Henry Graves establishes the Forest Service Branch of Research. In the following year, Graves directs experiment stations to focus specifically on fire research.

1922—Harry Gisborne transfers to the Priest River Experimental Forest in Idaho to initiate the Forest Service's first full-time fire research program.

1931—Harry Gisborne introduces the first Fire Danger Rating Meter, based on a Kodak Exposure Meter. For the light, exposure time, and aperture readings, Gisborne substituted fuel moisture, wind velocity, and relative humidity.

1934—Fire Danger Rating system developed by Harry Gisborne helps predict the Pete King-McLendon Butte fire, leading to a push for better weather data collection and fire management.

1935—Forest Service institutes the "quick-action strategy" (or ten o'clock rule) requiring that all fires "spotted in the course of a working day must be under control by ten o'clock the following morning."

1946—Forester Jack Barrows joins Harry Gisborne at Missoula and Priest River as the nation's second fulltime fire researcher at the Northern Rocky Mountain Research Station.

1949—Thirteen men are killed as a result of the Mann Gulch Fire near Helena, Montana. Three months later, Harry Gisborne, investigating the site of the fire, dies at the scene, in essence, the fourteenth casualty of the fire.

1952—Congress appropriates funds for a new Smokejumper Center west of Missoula, Montana, initiating a new Forest Service complex that would become home to the Northern Forest Fire Laboratory ("Fire Lab") in 1960.

1952—The movie "Red Skies of Montana," based on the tragedy of the Mann Gulch fire and starring Richard Widmark, released.

Coeur d'Alene National Forest after the 1910 fires (photo: USDA Forest Service).

The 1949 Mann Gulch from the air (photo: USDA Forest Service).

USDA Forest Service RMRS-GTR-270. 2012.

1953—Forest Service launches Project Skyfire, a collaborative research project with General Electric, to investigate methods to prevent or reduce the number of lightning-caused fires. Cloud seeding experiments initiated in 1956 as part of this research project. (This program was later cancelled because of inadvertent effects on the weather and farming.)

1954—Intermountain and Northern Rocky Mountain Research Stations merge, with headquarters for the region established in Ogden, Utah.

1957—Soviet Union launches Sputnik, resulting in a renewed U.S. commitment to science education and research.

1958—Congress appropriates funds for the Northern Forest Fire Laboratory, one of three regional wildland fire research facilities planned for the Forest Service (with facilities also designated for Riverside, California, and Macon, Georgia).

1958—First Fire Behavior Officers' training course, open to all agency personnel, offered at the Smoke Jumper Center in Missoula.

1960—The Northern Forest Fire Laboratory dedicated on September 12 in Missoula, Montana, by Forest Service Chief Richard McArdle and U.S. Representative, Lee Metcalf.

1961—Jack Barrows, Fire Lab Chief, hires several Idaho National Engineering Laboratory (INEL) researchers, including Richard Rothermel, Hal Anderson, and Stanley Hirsch as well as skilled technicians, Erv Breuer and Merlin Brown.

1962—Stanley Hirsch and his research team conduct one of the earliest tests of Project Fire Scan. Using a civilian version of infrared scanning for airborne fire detection, the researchers successfully mapped a 300-acre controlled burn 2,000 feet deep in a valley, where a temperature inversion had trapped a layer of smoke, obscuring visual detection.

1964—Jack Barrows promoted to head the Forest Service Fire and Atmospheric Science Research program in Washington, DC.

1964—The Wilderness Act designates an initial 9.1 million acres of national forests and wildlands as wilderness areas where "the earth and its community of life are untrammeled by man," where the "wilderness character" and integrity of the land are to be preserved, and forests and wildlands are allowed to change over time without interference.

Early fire danger rating signage (*photo: USDA Forest Service*).

Using a portable weather station to gather fire weather data during the 1959 Brackett Creek Fire in the Gallatin Natioinal Forest (*photo: USDA Forest Service*).

Mounting silver iodide generator for Project Skyfire, 1964 (*photo: USDA Forest Service*).

1966—William Beaufait, Charles (Mike) Hardy, and William (Bill) Fischer initiate one of the few large-scale controlled research projects at the 5,000 acre Miller Creek area in Montana on the effect of prescribed fire on air quality, vegetation development, conifer regeneration, water quality, erosion, and small animal populations.

1970—Fire Lab scientist Robert Mutch and Forest Service forester David Aldrich initiate a study of how to allow fire to assume its natural role in the national forests, particularly those designated as wilderness.

1972—Richard Rothermel publishes *"A Mathematical Model for Predicting Fire Spread in Wildland Fuels,"* a quantitative tool for predicting the spread and intensity of forest fires that continues to form the basis for fire behavior prediction and fire danger rating systems.

1972—John Deeming and others publish the *"National Fire-Danger Rating System,"* which is implemented nationally to "aid in planning and supervising fire control activities on a fire protection unit." The system was the first application of the Rothermel fire spread model as part of the basic platform of a national management tool.

1972—Fire scientist Robert Mutch and Forest Service employee Dave Aldrich complete their White Cap Fire Management Prescribed Natural Fire plan, which is approved by Forest Service Chief John McGuire and implemented successfully that summer. In August, a fire breaks out in Bad Luck Creek within the test area, and the decision is made to let it burn. The fire lasts 4 days and burns less than a quarter of an acre.

1974—Forest Service establishes the Fire in Multiple-Use Management Research, Development and Applications (RD&A) Program to improve the land manager's capability to integrate fire into land-use planning and management activities. Headed by Jim Lotan, this program initiated new research into fire as a way to meet objectives rather than just a force to be controlled.

1974—Jim Brown publishes "Handbook for inventorying downed woody material," which provides the foundation for quantitative measurement and analysis of wildland fuels.

1976—Frank Albini publishes his nomographs (also known as "nomograms"), visual calculating devices to help predict fire behavior in the field. Richard Rothermel described it as letting "the genie out of the bottle."

1976—Frank Albini, Hal Anderson, and Richard Rothermel develop and teach a new fire behavior officers' course at Marana, Arizona, for fire analysts from all Federal agencies using Rothermel's fire spread model and Albini's nomograms.

1977—Patricia (Pat) Andrews makes an initial presentation on the BEHAVE fire behavior prediction system, the first computerized system to incorporate many of the Fire Lab

Fire Lab education activities during 2004 open house (*photo: USDA Forest Service*).

Early field research with anenometers, 1962 (*photo: USDA Forest Service*).

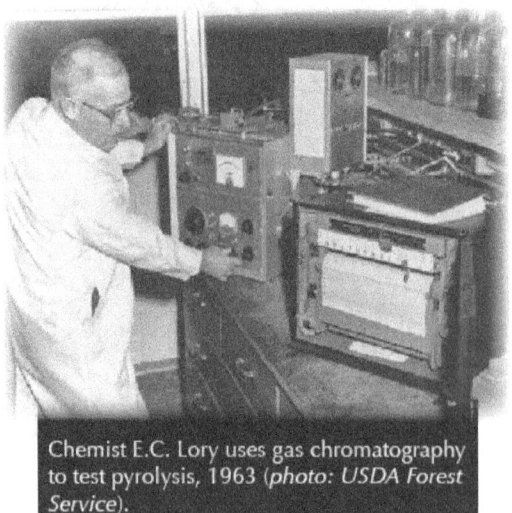

Chemist E.C. Lory uses gas chromatography to test pyrolysis, 1963 (*photo: USDA Forest Service*).

USDA Forest Service RMRS-GTR-270. 2012.

models. Because of insufficient computer capabilities in the field to run the program, however, the system was not available widely until 1984, when it was officially implemented nationwide.

1977—Researchers at the Fire Lab, including Jack Deeming, Bob Burgan, and Jack Cohen update the National Fire Danger Rating System. Fire managers use quantitative products from the system for planning. Descriptors ranging from low to extreme are communicated to the general public on Smokey Bear and other signage.

1978—The Forest Service officially ends the "10 a.m. rule" (or policy), allowing some fires on national forest lands to continue burning for "predetermined beneficial purposes." The name of the Division of Fire Control changes to the Division of Fire Management.

1979—Robert Burgan develops a pre-programmed chip to run on a TI-59 hand-held calculator, allowing managers to use the Rothermel model to calculate fire spread in the field. This new computer capability also enables managers to analyze prescribed burns and other proactive fire management activities.

1981—Bill Fischer publishes the first photo guides for appraising wildland fuels, which is an approach for field assessment of fuels that has been followed by dozens of publications nationwide.

1984—BEHAVE fire behavior prediction system is implemented nationwide.

1985—Jim Brown, Bill Fischer, and Cameron (Cam) Johnston initiate the Fire Effects Information System, a computer-based "encyclopedia" of effects of fire on plants and animals in North America. The system is moved to the Internet in 1994.

1987—The Fire Lab establishes a new Fire Chemistry research unit, with scientist Darold Ward appointed project leader. In 1989, the Forest Service moves its fire chemistry program from Macon, Georgia to the Missoula facility and, in 1991, Wei Min Hao joins the lab, to work on a major study of global air quality in partnership with NASA.

1988—Fires burn close to a million acres in Yellowstone National Park and lead fire researchers to develop additional models for fire behavior in extreme conditions.

1989—Forest Service moves its fire chemistry program from Macon, Georgia, to the Missoula Fire Lab.

1989—Bob Keane, Elizabeth Reinhardt, and Jim Brown introduce the first generation of FOFEM—the First Order Fire Effects Model—an easy-to-use software package that allows fire and land managers to predict, plan for, and quantify the immediate effects of fire.

1991—Wei Min Hao joins the Fire Lab, to work on a major study of global air quality in partnership with NASA.

1991—Richard Rothermel publishes "Predicting Behavior and Size of Crown Fires in the Northern Rocky Mountains," the result of research motivated in part by the 1988 Yellowstone fires.

Firefighter during 1988 Yellowstone National Fire (*photo: Jeff Henry, National Park Service*).

1994—The Fire Effects Information System is moved to the Internet.

1998—Mark Finney publishes FARSITE, a fire area simulator that integrates several fire models, improved visualization technology, and GIS data to calculate and visually display where a fire might grow and how quickly it might spread under changing terrain, fuels, and weather conditions.

2000—Jane Kapler Smith and Nancy McMurray complete the FireWorks educational trunk, providing educational materials and a fire-related curriculum tied to state and national science standards.

2002—Satellite receiving station added to the Fire Lab to download data on detected "hot spots" from two new satellites, sometimes as often as 12 times a day. Researchers compile this information with data collected on the ground, including reports of fire, to provide a more complete picture of atmospheric smoke and other pollutants. The resulting analyses also are used to predict air quality downwind from large fires across the continental United States.

2007—Fire Lab chemist, Wei Min Hao, a member of the Intergovernmental Panel on Climate Change, awarded the Nobel Peace Prize for the Panel's "efforts to build up and disseminate greater knowledge about man-made climate change, and to lay the foundations for the measures that are needed to counteract such change."

2008—Emily Heyerdahl, Penelope Morgan, and James Riser publish their study of the early fire histories of ponderosa pine forests of Idaho and western Montana (from 1650-1900). Their research is part of their larger study using fire scars and tree ring reconstructions to investigate climate drivers of fire in the Northern Rockies.

2009—A new addition to the Fire Lab, which houses administrative offices and the Fire Effects Library (more than 60,000 articles on ecology and fire effects) officially opens.

2010—Fire Sciences Laboratory in Missoula celebrates 50 years of research on September 18.

In 2010, the Fire Lab hosted an open house in celebration of its 50th anniversary (*photo: USDA Forest Service*).

Fire Lab retirees gather during the 50th anniversary in 2010 (*photo: USDA Forest Service*).

References

Albini, F. A. 1976. Estimating wildfire behavior and effects. Gen. Tech. Rep. INT-30. Ogden, UT: U.S. Department of Agriculture, Forest Service, Intermountain Forest and Range Experiment Station. 92 p.

Albini, F. A. 1984. Wildland fires. American Scientist. 72: 590-597.

Alexander, M. E.; Cruz, Miguel G.; Lopes, A. M. G. 2006. CFIS: a software tool for simulating crown fire initiation and spread. Forest Ecology Management. 234(S133).

Ambrosia, V. G.; Buechel, S. W.; Brass, J. A.; Peterson, J. R.; Davies, R. H.; Kane, R. J.; Spain, S. 1998. An Integration of remote sensing, GIS, and information distribution for wildfire detection and management. Photogrammetric Engineering & Remote Sensing. 64(10): 977-985.

Anderson, H. E. 1982. Aids to determining fuel models for estimating fire behavior. Gen. Tech. Rep. INT-122. Ogden, UT: U.S. Department of Agriculture, Forest Service, Intermountain Forest and Range Experiment Sation. 22 p.

Anderson, H. E.; Rothermel, R. C. 1965. Influence of moisture and wind upon the characteristics of free-burning fires. In: 10th Symposium (International) on Combustion; August 1964; Cambridge, England. Pittsburgh, PA: The Combustion Institute.

Andrews, P. 1986. Methods for predicting fire behavior—You do have a choice. Fire Management Notes. 47(2).

Andrews, P. 2006. Obituary, Frank Albini: 1936-2005. International Journal of Wildland Fire. 15: 1-2.

Andrews, P. 2007. BehavePlus fire modeling system: past, present, and future. In: Proceedings of 7th symposium on fire and forest meteorology; October 23-25, 2007; Bar Harbor, ME. Boston, MA: American Meteorological Society. 13 p.

Andrews, P. 2010. Personal communication. Research Physical Scientist, Missoula Fire Sciences Laboratory. Interview conducted by Diane Smith, April 1. Missoula, Montana.

Anjozian, L.-N. 2009. Lookouts in the sky with algorithms: Forecasting air quality with satellite-sent data. Fire Science Brief. 74. Online: http://www.firescience.gov/projects/briefs/01-1-5-03_FSBrief74.pdf.

Arno, S. F. 2010. Personal communication. Missoula Fire Sciences Laboratory ecologist, retired. Interview conducted by Diane Smith, April 2. Missoula, Montana.

Arno, S.; Allison-Bunnell, S. 2002. Flames in our forests: Disaster or renewal. Washington, DC: Island Press.

Arnold, K. 1964. Project Skyfire lightning research. In: Tall Timbers Fire Ecology conference proceedings. Tallahassee, FL: Tall Timbers Research Station: 122-123.

Bailey, D. W. 1979. Data processing: Customizing the calculator. Business Week. 2597: 66.

Barrows, J. S. 1951. Fire behavior in northern Rocky Mountain forests. Station Paper 29. Missoula, MT: U.S. Department of Agriculture, Forest Service, Northern Rocky Mountain Forest and Range Experiment Station. 103 p.

Barrows, J. S. 1958a. Fire fighting in laboratories. Talk delivered at Western Forest Fire Research Council meeting; December 9, 1958; San Francisco, CA. On file at: University of Montana, Mansfield Papers, Collection 65, box 69, folder 1.

Barrows, J. S. 1958b. They probe lightning fires. Western Conservation Journal. xv(1): 20-21, 42-43.

Barrows, J. S. 1959. Project Skyfire experiments with cloud seeding. Radio interview by reporter Laurie Corchin. Audio clip: http://archives.cbc.ca/science_technology/natural_science/topics/849-4927/. [April 12, 2011].

Barrows, J. S. 1971. Fire-fighting chemicals. In: Proceedings of a symposium on employment of air operations in the fire services; June 9-10, 1971; Argonne, IL. Washington, DC: National Academy of Sciences: 105-112.

Barrows, J. S. 1976. Harry T. Gisborne.Transcripts of interview conducted by C.E. Hardy with Jack Barrows; Feb. 26, 1976; Fort Collins, Colorado. On file at University of Montana, Missoula.

Barrows, J. S.; Deterich, J. H.; Odell, C. A.; and others. 1958. Project Skyfire. In: Final report of the advisory committee on weather control. Vol. II. Washington, DC: United States Congress, Advisory Committee on Weather Control: 105-125.

Barrows, J. S.; Schaefer, V.; MacCready, P. B., Jr. 1954. Project Skyfire: A progress report on lightning fire and atmospheric research. Res. Pap. INT-35. Ogden, UT: U.S. Department of Agriculture, Forest Service, Intermountain Forest and Range Experiment Station. 49 p.

Bartlette, Bobbie. 2010. Personal communication. Forester, retired, Missoula Fire Sciences Laboratory. Interview conducted by Diane Smith, January 26, Missoula, Montana.

Brinkley, D. 2009. The Wilderness Warrior: Theodore Roosevelt and the Crusade for America. New York, NY: Harper Collins Publishers. 960 p.

Brown, A. A.; Davis, W. S. 1939. A fire danger meter for the Rocky Mountain Region. Journal of Forestry. 37(7): 552-558.

Brown, J. 2010. Personal communication. Research Forester, retired, Missoula Fire Sciences Laboratory. Interview conducted by Diane Smith, April 8, , Missoula, Montana.

Brown, J. K. 1974. Handbook for inventorying downed woody material. Gen. Tech. Rep. INT-16. Ogden, UT: U.S. Department of Agriculture, Forest Service, Intermountain Forest and Range Experiment Station. 24 p.

Bunton, D. 2000. Wildland fire and weather information data warehouse. In: Seventh symposium on systems analysis in forest resources; 1997 May 28-31; Traverse City, MI. Gen. Tech. Rep. NC-205. St. Paul, MN: U.S. Department of Agriculture, Forest Service, North Central Forest Experiment Station. 7 p. Online: http://www.nrs.fs fed.us/pubs/gtr/other/gtr-nc205/pdffiles/p69.pdf. [Accessed January 29, 2010]

Burgan, R. E. 1979 Fire danger/ Fire behavior computations with the Texas Instruments TI-59 Calculator: User's manual. U.S. Department of Agriculture, Forest Service, Intermountain Research Station. Gen. Tech. Rep. INT-61. 34 p.

Burgan, R. 2010. Personal Communication. Research Forester, retired, Missoula Fire Sciences Laboratory. Interview conducted by Diane Smith, April 6, Missoula, Montana.

Carle, D. 2002. Burning questions: America's fight with nature's fire. Westport, CT: Praeger Publishers. 298 p.

Cliff, E. P. 1962. Report of the Chief of the Forest Service, 1961. Washington, DC, Government Printing Office.

Cliff, E. P. 1963. Report of the Chief of the Forest Service, 1962. Washington, DC, Government Printing Office.

Cliff, E. P. 1964. Report of the Chief of the Forest Service, 1963. Washington, DC, Government Printing Office.

Cliff, E. P. 1967. Report of the Chief of the Forest Service, 1966. Washington, DC, Government Printing Office.

Cliff, E. P. 1968. Report of the Chief of the Forest Service, 1967. Washington, DC, Government Printing Office.

Cohen, J. D.; Burgan, R. E. 1978. Hand-held calculator for fire danger/fire behavior. Fire Management Notes. 40(1).

Cones, G.; Keller, P. 2008. Managing naturally-ignited fire, yesterday, today and tomorrow. Tucson, AZ: National Advanced Fire and Resource Institute (NAFRI), Wildland Lessons Learned Center. 47 p. Also available online: http://www.wildfirelessons.net/Additional.aspx?Page=131.

Cronan, W. 2005. Interview. Pinchot and utilitarianism: What is the "Greatest Good"? The Greatest Good" A Forest Service centennial film; website. Online: http://www fs.fed.us/greatestgood/press/mediakit/facts/puinchiot.shtml. [May 24, 2011].

Deeming, J. E.; Burgan, R. E.; Cohen, J. D. The National Fire Danger Rating System, 1978. Gen. Tech. Rep. INT-39, Ogden, UT: U.S. Department of Agriculture, Forest Service, Intermountain Forest and Range Experiment Station. 63 p.

Deeming, John E.; Lancaster, J. W.; Fosberg, M. S.; Furman, R. W.; Schroeder, M. J. 1972. The National Fire-Danger Rating System. Res. Pap. RM-84, Fort Collins, CO: U.S. Department of Agriculture, Forest Service, Rocky Mountain Forest and Range Experiment Station. 165 p.

Egan, T. 2009. The Big Burn: Teddy Roosevelt and the fire that saved America. Boston, MA: Houghton Mifflin Harcourt. 324 p.

Finney, M. A. 1998. FARSITE: Fire Area Simulator—Model development and evaluation. Res. Pap.RMRS-RP-4. Ogden, UT: U.S. Department of Agriculture, Forest Service, Rocky Mountain Research Station. 47 p.

Fischer, W. C. 1981a. Photo guide for appraising downed woody fuels in Montana forests: Grand fir-larch-Douglas-fir, western hemlock, western hemlock-western redcedar, and western redcedar cover types. Gen. Tech. Rep. INT-96. Ogden, UT: U.S. Department of Agriculture, Forest Service, Intermountain Forest and Range Experiment Station. 53 p.

Fischer, W. C. 1981b. Photo guide for appraising downed woody fuels in Montana forests: Interior ponderosa pine, ponderosa pine–larch–Douglas-fir, larch–Douglas-fir, and interior Douglas-fir cover types. Gen. Tech. Rep. INT-97. Ogden, UT: U.S. Department of Agriculture, Forest Service, Intermountain Forest and Range Experiment Station. 133 p.

Fischer, W. C. 1981c. Photo guide for appraising downed woody fuels in Montana forests: Lodgepole pine, and Engelmann spruce–subalpine fir cover types. Gen. Tech. Rep. INT-98. Ogden, UT: U.S. Department of Agriculture, Forest Service, Intermountain Forest and Range Experiment Station. 143 p.

George, C. W. 1975. Fire Retardant Ground Distribution Patterns from the CL-215 Air Tanker. Res. Pap. INT-165. Ogden, UT: U.S. Department of Agriculture, Forest Service, Intermountain Forest and Range Experiment Station. 67 p.

George, C. W.; Fuchs, F. A. 1991. Improving airtanker delivery performance. Fire Management Notes. 52(2): 30-39.

Gisborne, H. T. 1941. An analysis of the forest fire problem in Regions I, II, III and IV. Missoula, MT: Northern Rocky Mountain Forest and Range Experiment Station, Fire, Problem Analysis.

Gisborne, H. T. 1948. Fundamentals of fire behavior. Fire Control Notes. 9(1): 13-24.

Graves, H. S. 1912a, The profession of forestry. Circular 207. Washington, DC: U.S. Department of Agriculture, Forest Service. 17 p.

Graves, H. S. 1912b. Report of the Forester for 1911. Washington, DC, Government Printing Office.

Graves, H. S. 1919. [Title not known]. Aviation Week, January 15, 1919: 113-114, 120. Quote from the Forest Service History site: http://www.fs.fed.us/aboutus/history/chiefs/graves.shtml.

Hardy, C. C. 2010. Personal communication. Program Manager, Missoula Fire Sciences Laboratory. Interview conducted by Diane Smith, March 30. Missoula, Montana.

Hardy, C. C.; Hardy, C. E. 2007. Fire danger rating in the United States of America: An evolution since 1916. International Journal of Wildland Fire. 16: 217-231.

Hardy, C. E. 1958. The proposed national fire danger rating system. In: 1958 National Meeting of the American Meteorology Society; Logan, UT. Washington, DC: American Meteorology Society.

Hardy, C. E. 1977. The Gisborne era of forest fire research. Completion Report. Missoula, MT: University of Montana, Forest and Conservation Experiment Station, in cooperation with U.S. Department of Agriculture, Forest Service.

Hardy, C. E. 2010. Personal communication. Forester, Missoula Fire Sciences Laboratory, retired. Interview conducted by Diane Smith, March 26. Missoula, Montana.

Hays, S. P. 1959, 1975. Conservation and the gospel of efficiency: The progressive conservation movement, 1890-1920. New York, NY: Atheneum.

Hirsch, S. N. 1971. Application of infrared scanners to forest fire detection. Paper presented at the International Remote Sensing Workshop, 1971, Ann Arbor, MI. 18 p. Online: http://nirops.fs fed.us/docs/about-more/06-Application%20of%20Infrared%20Scanners.pdf.

Hirsch, S. N. 1971. Fire intelligence. In: Employment of air operations in the fire services. Proceedings of a symposium; June 9-10, 1971; Argonne, IL. Washington, DC: National Academy of Sciences: 127-148.

Klade, R. J. 2006. Building a Research Legacy: The Intermountain Station, 1911-1997. Gen. Tech. Rep. RMRS-GTR-184. Fort Collins, CO: U.S. Department of Agriculture, Forest Service, Rocky Mountain Research Station. 259 p.

Koch, E. [n.d.]. History of the 1910 forest fires in Idaho and western Montana. Unpublished document on file at: University of Montana, Library, Government Collection, Missoula, MT.

Lassen, L. 2009. A historic look at the Intermountain Research Station. Online: http://www fs.fed.us/rmrs/about/history/. [Accessed 3/28/2011].

Lewis, J. G. 2006. The Forest Service and the greatest good: A Centennial History. Durham, NC: Forest History Society. 286 p.

Lotan, J. E. 1979. Integrating fire management into land-use planning: A multiple-use management research, development, and applications program. Environmental Management. 3(1): 7-14.

Maclean, N. 1992. Young men and fire. University of Chicago Press.

Mann, C. 2005. 1491: New revelations of the Americas before Columbus. New York, NY: Knopf. 465 p.

Mansfield, M. 1958. A Proposed Fire Laboratory for the Intermountain West.

McArdle, R. E. 1953. Report of the Chief of the Forest Service, 1952. Washington, DC, Government Printing Office.

McGuire, J. R. 1975. Report of the Chief of the Forest Service, 1974. Washington, DC, Government Printing Office.

Metcalf, L. 1958. Hearings before a subcommittee of the Committee on Appropriations, House of Representatives, Eighty-fifth Congress, Second Session; January 23, 1958. Missoula: Montana Historical Society, Lee Metcalf Collection 172: 902.

Mutch, R. W. 1970. Wildland fires and ecosystems—A hypothesis. Ecology. 51: 1046-1051.

Mutch, R. W. 2010. Personal communication. Fire scientist, Missoula Fire Sciences Laboratory (retired). Interview conducted by Diane Smith, March 30. Missoula, Montana.

National Park Service. 2008. The Yellowstone fires of 1988. Washington, DC: U.S. Department of the Interior, National Park Service. 7 p. http://www.nps.gov/yell/planyourvisit/upload/firesupplement.pdf [Accessed June 13, 2011].

Nelson, S.; Rollins, J. 1952. Smokey the bear. Song, written under license of the U.S. Dept. of Agriculture to Hill and Range Songs, Inc. Copyright 1952 by Hill and Range Songs, Inc., New York, N.Y.

New York Times. 1910. Government spends millions fighting forest fires: Small army of men employed to protect the reserves from devastations such as have been sweeping the West. August 28. Online: http://query.nytimes.com/gst/abstract.html?res=9D06E0D71E39E333A2575BC2A96E9C946196D6CF. [March 23, 2011].

Nobel Prize. 2007. The Nobel Peace Prize 2007. Nobelprize.org. Online: http://nobelprize.org/nobel_prizes/peace/laureates/2007. [Aug. 3, 2011].

Pinchot, G. 1899. Report of the Forester. In: Annual Reports of the Department of Agriculture, for the Fiscal Year Ending June 30, 1899," Washington, DC: Government Printing Office.

Pinchot, G. 1905. The 1905 "Use Book": The use of the National Forest Reserves: regulations and instructions. Washington, DC: U.S. Department of Agriculture, Forest Service. 80 p. Online: http://www foresthistory.org/ASPNET/publications/1905_Use_Book/1905_use_book.pdf. [February 28, 2010].

Pinchot, G. 1909. Primer of forestry, Part II practical forestry. Bulletin 24, Part II. Washington, DC: U.S. Department of Agriculture, Bureau of Forestry. Online: https://fp.auburn.edu/sfws/sfnmc/class/pinchot html. [March 28, 2011].

Pyne, S. J. 1997. America's fires: management on wildlands and forests. Durham, NC: Forest History Society.

Pyne, S. J. 2001. Year of the fires : The story of the great fires of 1910. New York, NY: Viking. 321 p.

Robbins, W. G. 1984. Federal forestry cooperation—The Fernow-Pinchot years. Journal of Forest History. 28(4): 164-173.

Roosevelt, T. December 3, 1901. First annual message to the Senate and House of Representatives. State of the Union Address. American Presidency Project. Online: http://www.presidency.ucsb.edu/ws/index.php?pid=29542#axzz1HvZsfSJA [January 9, 2010].

Rothermel, R. C. 1972. A mathematical model for predicting fire spread in wildland fuels. Res. Pap. INT-115. Ogden, UT: U.S. Department of Agriculture, Forest Service, Intermountain Forest and Range Experiment Station. 40 p.

Rothermel, R. C. 1983. How to predict the spread and intensity of forest and range fires. Gen. Tech. Rep. INT-143. Ogden, UT: U.S. Department of Agriculture, Forest Service, Intermountain Forest and Range Experiment Station. 161 p.

Rothermel, R. C. 1991. Predicting behavior and size of crown fires in the northern Rocky Mountains. Res. Pap. INT-438. Ogden UT: U.S. Department of Agriculture, Forest Service, Intermountain Research Station. 46 p.

Rothermel, R. C. 1993. Mann Gulch fire: A race that couldn't be won. Gen. Tech. Rep. 299. Ogden, UT: U.S. Department of Agriculture, Forest Service, Intermountain Research Station. 10 p. Online: http://www.fs fed.us/rm/pubs_int/int_gtr299.pdf.

Rothermel, R. C. 2010. Personal communication. Engineer, Missoula Fire Sciences Laboratory, retired. Interview Conducted by Diane Smith, April 6, Missoula, Montana.

Schaefer, V. and C. E. Hardy 1976. Personal communication. Interview with Harry Gisborne conducted by Vince Schaefer, June 20, 1976. On file at University of Montana Library, OH-44-7, Missoula, MT.

Sikkink, P. G.; Lutes, D. C.; Keane, R. E. 2009. Field guide for identifying fuel loading models. Gen. Tech. Rep. RMRS-GTR-225. Fort Collins, CO: U.S. Department of Agriculture, Forest Service, Rocky Mountain Research Station. 33 p.

Silcox, F. A. 1935. Report of the Chief of the Forest Service, 1935. Washington, DC, Government Printing Office.

Smith, J. K. 2010. Personal communication. Ecologist, and FEIS Manager, Missoula Fire Sciences Laboratory. Interview Conducted by Diane Smith, April 22, Missoula, Montana.

Smith, J. K. and N. E. McMurray. 2000. FireWorks curriculum featuring ponderosa, lodgepole, and whitebark pine forests. Gen. Tech. Rep. RMRS-GTR-65. Fort Collins, CO: U.S. Department of Agriculture, Forest Service, Rocky Mountain Research Station. 270 p.

Steen, H. K. 1976, 2004. The U.S. Forest Service: A History. Seattle, WA: University of Washington Press. 432 p.

Stilling, D. 2005. Forests, fires & elk: Logging for healthy habitat? Boise, ID: Idaho Forest Products Commission. [May 6, 2010]. Online: http://www.idahoforests.org/elk.htm.

USDA Forest Service. 1957. A proposed Forest Fire Laboratory for the Intermountain West . Ogden, UT: U.S. Department of Agriculture, Forest Service, Intermountain Forest and Range Experiment Station. On file at: University of Montana, Mansfield papers VIII, box 15, folder 6, Missoula, MT.

USDA Forest Service, 1960. Dedication brochure. Missoula, MT: The Northern Forest Fire Laboratory: 3.

Watts, L. F. 1949. Report of the Chief of the Forest Service, 1949. Washington, DC, Government Printing Office.

Watts, L. F. 1951. Report of the Chief of the Forest Service, 1951. Washington, DC, Government Printing Office.

Wells, G. 2008. The Rothermel fire-spread model: Still running like a champ. Fire Science Digest.. 2. Online: http://www.firescience.gov/Digest/FSdigest2.pdf. [March 28, 2011].

Wells, G. 2009. Wildland fire use: Managing for a fire-smart landscape. Fire Sciences Digest. 4. Online: http://www.firescience.gov/Digest/FSdigest4.pdf. [March 28, 2011].

Wellner, C. A. 1976. Frontiers of forestry research: Priest River Experimental Forest, 1911-1976. Ogden, UT: U.S. Department of Agriculture, Forest Service, Intermountain Forest and Range Experiment Station. 148 p.

West, T. 1992. The Weeks Act and eastern forests. Chapter 16. In: Centennial mini-histories of the Forest Service. FS-518. Durham, NC: The Forest History Society. Online: http://www.foresthistory.org/ASPNET/Publications/centennial_minis/chap16.htm[January 10, 2010].

Wilson, R. A.; Nost, N. V. 1966. Project fire scan; fire detection interim report, April 1962 to December 1964. Res. Pap. INT-25. Ogden, UT: U.S. Department of Agriculture, Forest Service, Intermountain Forest and Range Experiment Station. 55 p.